The Fables of

AESOP

with Designs on Wood by Thomas

BEWICK

The Fables of

AESOP

with Designs on Wood by Thomas

BEWICK

**with a
new introduction by
Michael Marqusee**

**PADDINGTON
Masterpieces of the
Illustrated Book**

**TWO CONTINENTS
PUBLISHING GROUP**

Library of Congress Cataloging in Publication Data
Aesopus.
The fables of Aesop.
(Masterpieces of the illustrated book)
Reprint of the 1818 ed. printed by
E. Walter, Newcastle, for T. Bewick.
1. Fables. I. Bewick, Thomas, 1753-1828.
PA3855.E5B38 1975   398.2'452   75-11176

ISBN 0–8467–0076–X
Library of Congress Catalog Card Number 75–11176
Copyright 1975 Paddington Press Ltd
Printed in the U.S.A.

IN THE UNITED STATES
PADDINGTON PRESS LTD
TWO CONTINENTS PUBLISHING GROUP
30 East 42 Street
New York City, N.Y. 10017

IN THE UNITED KINGDOM
PADDINGTON PRESS LTD
231 The Vale
London W3

IN CANADA
distributed by
RANDOM HOUSE OF CANADA LTD
5390 Ambler Drive, Mississauga
Ontario L4W 1Y7

INTRODUCTION

Thomas Bewick was known to a large public as the preeminent
wood-engraver and one of the foremost illustrators of his day. Since then,
however, few besides antiquarians and enthusiasts have taken an interest in his
work. Bibliophiles have collected his blocks and his books, scholars (and some
rather unscholarly enthusiasts) have compiled bibliographies, but few critics
have evaluated his art as a significant and potentially popular collection of
images. In the later nineteenth century, J. W. Linton, at that time a leading
engraver and illustrator, looked back to Bewick rather as a founding father of
the trade than as an artist. And Austin Dobson's Victorian study of *Bewick and
His School* has a patronizing air reminiscent of Elizabethan criticism of Chaucer.
For these men Bewick was primarily a technical innovator, and they were
charmed mainly by what they considered the quaint, rustic qualities of his art.
Ruskin fell into a different kind of error when he compared Bewick's "bitter
intensity of feeling" to "that which characterizes some of the leading
pre-Raphaelites."

Yet who today cares about the antiquated judgments of a Linton or a Dobson,
even a Ruskin, and why invoke them in the beginning of a new discussion of
Bewick's work? The answer is that these Victorian attitudes still prevail in many
quarters and that Bewick's work is still little known outside bibliophilic circles
and little appreciated within them (see David Bland's *A History of Book
Illustration*, pp. 222-227). His finest creations offer a visual and intellectual

pleasure not to be drawn from any of the art that surrounds us today; yet they remain so accessible and unforbidding that it is a shame a wider public has not had an opportunity to know them. Hence this Paddington Press edition, the first of Bewick's illustrated books to be made generally available in its original format since the Memorial editions of 1885.

"To see something new we must make something new." Lichtenberg's aphorism is demonstrated quite literally by the coincidence in Bewick's career of technical and artistic developments. The invention of wood-engraving is often ascribed to him, but it seems more likely that it was already in use by provincial craftsmen in 1767, when Bewick was apprenticed at the age of fourteen to Ralph Beilby, a Newcastle artisan. Wood-cutting, the predecessor of wood-engraving, had been the dominant medium of illustration throughout the sixteenth century and was gradually replaced in the seventeenth by copper-plate engraving, which was in turn supplemented by various etching processes. The wood-engraving in the eighteenth century was used for simple linear designs in chapbooks, posters, and other cheap and popular productions. Bewick's master had neither facility nor interest in the medium and delegated these commissions to his apprentice. Briefly stated, the difference between wood-cutting and wood-engraving is as follows. In wood-cutting, the artist removes the spaces that are to print white (that is, not to print at all) with a knife or chisel and cuts with the grain on a plank that is itself cut with the grain (vertically). In wood-engraving the artist uses a burin or small-pointed engraving tool (similar to those used on copper or steel) to remove the white spaces, and he works on a surface of hard wood cut across the grain (horizontally). The latter process tends to produce a finer white line and permits greater precision and density of detail. Its line is softer than metal-plate engravings and cleaner than etchings. Bewick was the first to exploit these advantages, and through his work the medium gained ascendancy in book-illustration (at least in England) until the advent of photomechanical processes in the late nineteenth century.

It is significant that when Bewick demonstrated a proclivity for drawing, or "imitating nature" as he called it, his parents would think of the Beilby shop as a logical training ground. Beilby offered a variety of services to his neighbors in the middle and upper classes: coffin plates, settings for jewels or watches. This was an environment untouched by the fitful ruptures between artist and patron and public that had become a regular feature of artistic life in the remote centers of London and Paris. In shops like Beilby's the struggle between commercial and aesthetic requirements was lived through on a day by day, job by job basis.

And it was one in which the commercial inevitably triumphed.

It would be wrong, however, to think that Bewick was apprenticed to a tradition that merely subordinated beauty to utility. Anyone who has ever poured tea from a fine old teapot or stored trinkets in an ornamented box knows the pleasure of discovering a modest beauty in the midst of the necessary affairs of life. When such objects were the manufacture of contemporaries, perhaps of a neighbor or acquaintance, the pleasure must have been that much more intimate. Because these things were not set apart from the intercourse of daily life they embellished that life in a way that self-professed works of art, for all that they teach and give to the inner life, cannot.

This tradition marks Bewick's art in two ways. The first is his devotion to the illustrated book. He produced no important work outside this medium. There is a special delight, which I hope the owner of this volume will come to know, in finding these rich and highly finished works of art not on a museum wall but in a book which one can live with and open at leisure. And one can be alone with an illustrated book as with none of the other visual arts. The second is Bewick's belief in the utility of art (see p.xvi of his introduction). Of course, the kind of utility he meant was moral, not practical. But it is linked to the practical values of the Beilby shop in that it never substituted the abstraction of virtue for the thing itself; it never confused instruction with the inculcation of prejudice. His craftsmanship served his moral purpose by enabling people to see clearly and proportionally. How different are these values from those of the crafts movement of the later nineteenth century, or from those of the resurgence of this movement that we are witnessing today.

Bewick's childhood on a prosperous Northumberland farm was the other factor which, along with the traditions of his apprenticeship, determined the direction of his art. He has described it in his *Memoir,* a self-portrait as unpretentious and winning as its author's designs, which was finished shortly before his death and published by his daughter many years later. The vividly recollected scenes of its opening chapters show that after a lifetime of stern workmanship Bewick was still able to enjoy the episodes, impressions, and pranks of his school days. Like Wordsworth, he found creative sustenance in his memories of secluded rural scenes and eighteenth-century village life, both of which had ceased to exist by the time he was middle-aged. Indeed, one of the pleasures of the *Memoir* is its picture of the pre-industrial north of England. Bewick lived and worked in Newcastle for the majority of his years, yet in only a handful of his designs can there be found any vestige of urban life. The incidents of the farm and the village green, the woods and streams, above all, the animals and birds – these are the subjects to which Bewick applied his imagination over and over again throughout his career, always in the same diminutive monochromatic form and, astonishingly, without ever exhausting or repeating himself. In this way he created an integral artistic world out of the memory of a real one which had vanished. The remarkable thing is that he did this with only rare forays into sentimentality or caricature (both prevalent modes in nineteenth-century book illustration). One therefore feels comfortable in this world without feeling coddled; in perusing any of his major books one finds oneself on safe but always surprising ground.

Bewick's first engravings were illustrations of *Gay's Fables*. These are for the most part simple line drawings with little gradation of texture, executed while he was still an apprentice. One of them, "The Old Hound," won him a premium of seven guineas from the Society for the Encouragement of the Arts. In this work Bewick shows for the first time his ability to organize a complex action within a small space. And it is the beginning of his campaign against cruelty to animals. After finishing his apprenticeship he spent a last idyllic year on his parents' farm, walked through the highlands of Scotland (one of the most exuberant chapters in the *Memoir* is devoted to this), and settled in London for six months where his engraving was praised and he received many commissions. He returned to Newcastle and formed a partnership with Beilby, taking in his younger brother John as an apprentice. The *Selected Fables*, with designs based on Croxall's edition of fifty years before, which were in turn based on previous editions, was published in 1784. Bewick does not mention this book in the *Memoir*, and it is thought that his brother and possibly others contributed to it. Whatever the case it does include designs in which the traditional materials are handled with shades of feeling not to be found in earlier engravings.

In 1785, Bewick's father, mother, and sister died. In the same year he began work on *The History of Quadrupeds*, the first book he executed from a conception of his own, and the first of his major achievements. The connection between these events is too obvious to be belabored. The book was an immediate success when finally published in 1790: it went through three editions in as many years and eight by the time of the artist's death. One reason for its success was that it established a definitive style for the wood-engraved illustration. Close parallel lines were used to suggest shades ranging from ink black to paper white. Where an impression of distance was required the surface of the block was lowered so that it would print paler. And Bewick had mastered the mixture of detail and clarity which was to characterize the "look" of the wood-engraving for decades to come.

Moreover, the economy with which he could present a complex incident or subtle emotion was displayed in the first of his famous tail-pieces. His sense of humor, his feeling for distance and varieties of weather, his restrained pathos made each of them (*tale*-pieces he called them) an environment in miniature. No wonder it was a success: the appeal of the book was unaffected and consistent; its technique was as sophisticated as its style was ingenuous.

Bewick's next major undertaking, the two volumes of *British Birds,* was received with even greater enthusiasm. He worked on it through the 1790's and into the first years of the new century, bringing out the *Land Birds* in 1797 and the *Water Birds* in 1804. What startled the public then was the incredible variety of tones and textures which Bewick had achieved without departing from the elementary methods of wood-engraving. Indeed, a book printed entirely in black that nonetheless manages to distinguish the color, shape and feeling of every feather of every bird ought still to excite our wonder today.

Aside from its technical achievements, *British Birds* demonstrates that Bewick was not only an accurate observer of nature, but a profound one. There is nothing "pretty" or anthropoid about these creatures; his fascination with them was not that of Shelley for the skylark or Keats for the nightingale. For Bewick their world was a heedless, volatile one, loved for its variety and drama. The stiffness that mars some of the quadrupeds is gone. He refused to draw from stuffed specimens and either waited for a freshly killed one or carried his blocks into the local aviaries and even into the forest:

> Had I been a painter, I never would have copied the works of 'old masters', or others, however highly they might be esteemed. I would have gone to nature for all my patterns: for she exhibits an endless variety not possible to be surpassed, and scarcely ever to be truly imitated.

The tail-pieces in the *Birds* explore even more inventively the vein first mined in the *Quadrupeds.* Here we find the visual equivalent of Wordsworth's simple but powerful rhetoric; this is everyday language used in the presentation of everyday subjects, expunged of the banal, the maudlin, the patronizing. Nothing in this book is tired or perfunctory. It went through six editions in his lifetime, some of them supplemented with new designs, and three after his death.

The *Birds* and the *Quadrupeds* made Bewick a famous man. His apprentices included such talented artisans as Luke Clennell, Charlton Nesbit, William Harvey, and John Jackson, all of whom went on to profitable careers as illustrators after their term with Bewick. They assisted their master in the execution of the many commissions he received from all over the country, cutting blocks from his designs as well as contributing designs of their own. There is no reason that this pooling of labor should make us distrust Bewick's later work. Although his art is always recognizably his own, it was never intended as an "expression of his personality", a dubious idea in any context, and should not be taken that way. When his commissioned work shows only technical excellence, it is not because his apprentices shared or even dominated the labor, but because the subject did not arouse Bewick's interest, which would have been manifest no matter how much assistance he received. This attitude is quite in keeping with the traditions of the Beilby shop; it must be remembered that Bewick never ceased to regard himself as a provincial artisan, engaged in the *business* of engraving on wood. When Dr. Thornton, who commissioned Blake to illustrate his textbook Virgil, asked Bewick to illustrate his *Herbal,* Bewick explained to Thornton that he took no interest in the subject, but would accept the assignment anyway. Consequently the book is not one of his major achievements (it has no tail-pieces), but it does include many fine examples of his technique and has become, like everything that Bewick touched, a collector's item.

More satisfying were the commissions he received from his friend William Bulmer, of the Shakespeare Printing Office in London. The most important of these is the *Goldsmith and Parnell* volume of 1795, with designs by both Bewick brothers. This was a conscious attempt to raise the level of English printing, and it stands today as one of the finest books of its time. Among the books for which he executed frontispieces or occasional illustrations are editions of Thomson's *Seasons* 1805 (one of his favorite poems), an anthology called *The Hive* 1806, Burns' *Poems* 1808, Ferguson's *Poems* 1814, and a wonderful set of the street-criers of Newcastle. In addition to his work for books, he cut many calling cards, labels, and invitations; one of his projects was to design a note for the Bank of England that could not be counterfeited, but his proposals were ignored.

Bewick's way of life in all these years remained unchanged. He believed strongly in the virtues of hard work and was scrupulous in meeting his obligations. At the same time he sustained many friendships with people of every degree, enjoyed good food and fireside family gatherings, and delighted in the idiosyncrasies of his native region: the old ballads, the bagpipe music, the retired soldiers, and the still-prevalent superstitions. He was an avowed Whig who maintained a lifelong interest in politics and concern for social justice. He sided with the American colonies in their struggle with the British government, deplored his country's participation in the Napoleonic wars, and expressed on many occasions his horror at the uselessness and waste of war in general. He protested the abuse of wealth and privilege, condemned those who profited from war or economic hardship, and advocated greater care in the exploitation of natural resources. He believed in God but opposed sectarianism of any kind, and found the doctrine of original sin completely unacceptable. The remarkable thing is that he arrived at these advanced ideas without a higher education or the influence of a sophisticated circle of friends. They were the product of an intelligent mind examining without prejudice the social conditions of the day, with constant reference to the values of communal cooperation he had learned in his youth. His manner of thinking may be observed in his original fable "The Ship Dog" (p. 99); the reader should bear in mind that it was written within a few years of the Battle of Waterloo.

Bewick began the *Fables of Aesop* after a long illness in 1812:

While I lay helpless from weakness, and pined to a skeleton, without any hopes of recovery being entertained by myself or anyone else, I became, as it were, all mind and memory. I had presented to my recollection almost everything that had passed through my life, both what I had done and what I had left undone. ... I could not ... help regretting that I had not published a book similar to Croxall's *Aesop*'s Fables, as I had always intended to do. I was extremely fond of that book; and, as it had afforded me much pleasure, I thought, with better executed designs, it would impart the same kind of delight to others as I had experienced while attentively reading it.

In this passage we can see how Bewick's need to summarize his personal experience mingles comfortably with his affection for a tradition. And this coupling of the personal and traditional accounts for many of *Aesop's* unusual features. To begin with, there is the colophon, designed by Bewick to insure against illegal sales. The colophon in this volume bears Bewick's actual signature, while the signature of his son is in facsimile. The seaweed was printed in brown from a copper-plate over the background, which was printed from a normal wood-block. Then there is the introduction, well worth reading, in which Bewick explains his intentions and states his admiration for the great fabulists of the past and present. These men are further memorialized in a series of tail-pieces scattered throughout the book, each with an appropriate set of props and often adorned with foliage, children, or animals; their work, for Bewick, has almost the permanence of nature, and a perpetual innocence denied to the individual man. Side by side with these emblems of tradition we find pieces inscribed with the dates of the deaths of his mother (p. 162) and his father

(p. 176). Only someone familiar with Bewick's biography (and the *Memoir* was published forty years after *Aesop*) could know the meaning of these dates; their very anonymity gives to the personal act of remembrance a strange universality. A similar quality is found in the tail-pieces which incorporate various mottoes and sayings into natural settings. In leafing through this book crammed with illustrations and incidents, these reflections strike us as sign-posts encountered periodically during a long journey. They are the offspring of Bewick's belief that the ways of nature and the wisdom of man are in harmony, and also of his delight in manipulating the different elements of the printed book. Two of these pieces deserving particular notice are on pages 28 and 62. In the former, two boys stare in awe at one of Bewick's favorite mottoes engraved on a cliff, while a tiny horseman, as if in demonstration of this "bold peasantry", crosses a bridge in the background. In the latter, the rain-streaked atmosphere reinforces the desolate, chilling motto (with I will not quote because it is much more effective in context).

The relationship of the vignettes to the fables they illustrate is another feature which makes the book far more than just an 'Aesop with illustrations'. The selection of fables is Bewick's own, and he wrote many of the applications, but in illustrating them he adheres to the dramatic incident itself; he strives for the most part to keep the visual material free of the moral. In some instances, such as "The Husbandman and the Stork" (p. 345) or "The Collier and the Fuller" (p. 13), his treatment implies a moral quite different from the written one. In general, the moral atmosphere of Bewick's applications is more stringent than that of his images, but this does not mean that we should discount one in favor of the other, or that there is any inconsistency in the book's purpose. It is part of a tendency which can also be seen in the variety of genres found in the tail-pieces. Some of these have already been mentioned. Others include the emblems of the butcher ('Bloodo et Gutto') on page 154 and of the city of Newcastle on page 106, and the pieces on pages 36, 76, 138, and 290, which are humorously commented upon in Bewick's own handwriting. Because so many of the vignettes contain material Bewick reserved in his previous books for tail-pieces, he seems in *Aesop* to have felt freer to experiment with the device than before. The images offer a virtual resumé of his life and work: cruelty to animals, the folly and mortality of man, the strange worlds of children and animals, the change of seasons, the repose of solitude. The whole book in fact constitutes a survey of life which is at once a *vanitas* and a *carpe diem*. One of the first pieces in the book shows an ape in the artist's studio drawing pictures of the other animals and the last a funeral (said to be his brother John's), and the contrast between wit and solemnity is characteristic of the book as a whole. It is the product of an individual sensibility deeply attached to tradition, of one who had in his life both enjoyed and regretted much.

And yet it has been denigrated ever since its publication. Even Bewick was disappointed: "I found in this book more difficulties to conquer that I had experienced with either the *Quadrupeds* or the *Birds* ... it was not so well printed as I had expected and wished." Years of working over small blocks, often by candlelight, had weakened his eyesight, and he states explicitly in the *Memoir* that he was assisted in *Aesop* by his son Robert, William Harvey, and William Temple. Much confusion has been caused by a story circulated by John Jackson, a former apprentice known to have feuded with Bewick, that the original designs for *Aesop* were all the work of Robert Johnson, an apprentice who died in 1796. This unlikely story, together with Bewick's own statements about the quality of printing and his need for assistance, has led many Bewick admirers, from Dobson to Philip Hofer, to dismiss Aesop as a second-rate production. It is true that the first edition was poorly printed, and it is still frustrating that so many of the designs are marred by sloppy inking. Nonetheless, it is included in Stanley Morison's *Four Centuries of Fine Printing* and in general design is one of the most attractive of Bewick's books. That he was closely involved in every stage of the book's conception and execution, except the actual printing, is evinced in countless details. That his work here is stiff or strained, as both Dobson and Hofer insist, is belied in design after design. In contrast to the *Quadrupeds* or *Birds*, *Aesop* is a late work, often indifferent to minor elegances, but the cuts in the *Memoir* are later still, and they are more often criticized for looseness than severity.

What, then, are the characteristics of Bewick's art in this book? In the tail-pieces, as usual, he presents common or simple occurrences from a distance that reveals in them intriguing and unexpected qualities. A boy propelling a sail-boat with a bellows (p. 140), an ox looking over a fence at a sleeping human couple (p. 341), a man on a horse wading through a stream (p. 132), a blind man guided by a dog (p. 204): in these and others it is his quiet curiosity, not detachment or "intensity of feeling," that Bewick transmits to us. In the horse waiting for death (p. 334) it is his respectfulness. In the drunk seeing two moons (p. 242) it is his gentle humor. In the angling pieces it is his love of the sport. Unfortunately there is only one good example in this book (p. 54) of a Bewick snowscape; but it is enough to show his ability to conjure a cold, thick blanket of snow from a ground of plain white paper. Look at the tail-piece of the wind blowing over a cliff on page 48: Bewick has suggested an elemental force in a limited space by the simple invention of having the girls hold on to their skirts like sails.

In the vignettes there is a similar conjunction of invention and economy. Although the subjects are predetermined, and in some cases the designs as well, things are nevertheless always presented in a novel and significant way. Schematic or geometrical compositions are avoided, and Bewick displays in almost every one his uncanny ability to enlarge a small space by the arrangement of forms within it. In "The Wolf and the Lamb" (p. 191) a stream winds through a forest filled with vegetation, the animals gingerly maneuver around its banks, the sun is seen through the trees; yet the effect is neither cluttered nor diffuse. Bewick rarely focuses our attention in the center of the image. He likes to create secondary points of interest and to distribute the action between foreground and background. In "The Hawk and the Farmer" (p. 329), the main action (and what justice he does to its violence!) takes place in the foreground on the left while the eye is led by the dog and the gate to an attractive background on the right. Our attention is always solicited by more than one element in the composition. Foliage and the contours of the countryside are used to make smaller frames which place these elements in proportional and dramatic relationship within the larger frame. Bewick often creates a 'keyhole' effect of looking through a small opening into a larger space, of looking into a clearing from the forest, which allows the eye to explore the scene intimately while remaining at a safe distance.

What we discover in this scene is usually a fine example of Bewick's observant draughtsmanship. Admittedly, he is not at his best when drawing animals, such as monkeys or tigers, which he had only seen in books. On the other hand, look at the "The Stag Looking into the Water" (p. 19) or the boar in "The Fox and the Boar" (p. 175). The stag is lithe and furry, it turns its head to gaze in the water with naive surprise; the boar is bulky, bristly, and fierce. And there is a strange pleasure in seeing such large animals rendered in such a small space. It is hard to say what in Bewick's drawing makes the simplicity of such compositions as "The Crow and the Pitcher" (p. 67) or "The Peacock and the Crane" (p. 23) so riveting; harder still to say how that simplicity manages to exert such an enduring fascination. Something in the way the animals are posed and arranged seems to suggest all that has come before and all that will follow the moment of illustration. And his skill is not restricted to the animal kingdom. The two men in "The Lark and her Young Ones" (p. 41) are without physical beauty and are doing nothing of particular interest, yet there is an unaffected certainty in Bewick's line that gives them an immediate appeal. His classical deities have been criticized, but I think for the most part they possess just the right degrees of shadow and substance, and their confrontations with mortal beings in "Mercury and the Woodsman" (p. 49) and "Jupiter and the Ass" (p. 79) inspire two of Bewick's best designs.

Aesop's Fables was published in 1818. In the years following Bewick worked intermittently on blocks for a book on British Fishes, but he seems never to have seriously pursued it, and the few he did finish were appended to the first edition of the *Memoir*. According to his family, "his chief delight [was] in throwing off subjects of fancy for his tail-pieces." These last pieces can also be found in the *Memoir*. They have a boldness, almost a wildness of imagination that one would expect to find in the work of a precocious child; Bewick could still see new possibilities in the wood-engraving fifty years after having first taken it up. He was one of those rare artists who are completely at home in a single medium. When he died in 1828 his blocks were already collector's items and his illustrations were appearing in unauthorized editions. All the engravers of the nineteenth century learned from his technique; but no subsequent illustrator of books in England has sustained a vision of comparable profundity.

Michael Marqusee

Newcastle 1st October 1818

To Thomas Bewick & Son Dr.

To an Impl. Copy of Esop's Fables $\frac{£}{1}$ " $\frac{s}{11}$ " $\frac{d}{6}$

Received the above with thanks

Thomas Bewick,   Robert Elliot Bewick

Thomas Bewick

his   Mark

THE

FABLES OF ÆSOP,

AND OTHERS,

WITH DESIGNS ON WOOD,

BY

THOMAS BEWICK.

" The wisest of the Ancients delivered their Conceptions of the Deity, and their Lessons of Morality, in Fables and Parables."

NEWCASTLE:

PRINTED BY E. WALKER, FOR T. BEWICK AND SON.
SOLD BY THEM, LONGMAN AND CO. LONDON,
AND ALL BOOKSELLERS.

1818,

Wise Men think
Good men Grieve
Knaves invent
and Fools believe.

THE PREFACE DEDICATORY.

To the Youth of the British Isles.

In collecting together, for your use and benefit, some of the prudential maxims, and moral apothegms, of the ancient sages, the Publishers of this volume have been stimulated by an ardent desire to render this excellent mode of instruction as agreeable as possible; and, at the same time, to impress the precepts contained in the Fables more forcibly on your minds, they have endeavoured to make the embellishments worthy of your notice and examination.

If the seeds of morality and patriotism be early sown, they will spring up, and ripen to maturity, in a confirmed love of truth, integrity and honour; and without these for his guide, no man can do credit to himself or his country. This consideration is of vital importance; for our comfort and happiness through life, mainly depend upon a strict adherence to the rules of morality and religion. The youth who is early tutored in an invincible regard for his own character, will soon perceive the duties imposed upon him by society, and will have pleasure in fulfilling them, as much for his own satisfaction as for the sake of his fellow men: but when the latent powers of the mind are neglected, or not directed into the paths of rectitude, by good precepts and worthy examples, vice and folly enter the opening, and lead their victim into evils and errors, which render his life miserable, and sometimes hurry him into an ignominious grave.

To delineate the characters and passions of men, under the semblance of Lions, Tigers, Wolves, and Foxes, is not so extravagant a fiction as it may at first sight seem: for the innocent and inexperienced will find, when they engage in the busy scenes of the world, that they will have to deal with men of dispositions not unlike those animals; and that their utmost vigilance will be required to guard against their violence or machinations.

In attempting to form an estimate of the characters of mankind, many gradations and shades will be found between the two extremes of virtue and vice. The philanthropist views with feelings of benevolence the wavering balance, and adds those he finds on the con-

fines, to the number of the virtuous; while the misanthrope, with gloomy malignity, endeavours to include
within the circle of vice, those who are standing upon
the ill-defined line of division, and thus swells the number of the bad. Both observe with pain, that great
numbers exist, whose whole lives seem to be spent in
disfiguring the beautiful order which might otherwise
reign in society, regardless of the misery which their
wickedness scatters around them. They see men, who
suffer their bad passions and gross appetites to be the
sole rule of their conduct; and whether these shew
themselves in an inordinate ambition, a thirst after false
glory, or an insatiable avarice, their consequences are
pernicious, and diffuse evil, distress, and ruin among
mankind, in proportion to the extent to which their
baneful influence reaches. The misanthrope, in contemplating the scene of mischief and disorder, is apt to
arraign the wisdom and justice of Providence for per-
mitting it to exist; but the philanthropist views it
with a more extended range of vision; and while he
laments the evil, he attributes the apparent want of
human feelings in the actors, to an early perversion of
intellect, or to a stifling of the reasoning power given
by the Great Creator to man for his guide, and without which he is the worst animal in the creation, a
mere two-legged Tiger. Upon the childhood and
youth of such men, the great truth taught by the in-

spired and wisest writers of all ages, that "no life can be pleasing to God which is not useful to man," has not been sufficiently impressed, or probably the energy with which they pursue their wicked career might have been led into a different course, and instead of the scourges, they would have been the benefactors of mankind.

When religion and morality are blended together in the mind, they impart their blessings to all who seek the aid of the one and obey the dictates of the other, and their joint effects are seen and felt in the perpetual cheerfulness they impart. They incite the innocent whistle of the ploughman at his plough, of the cobler in his stall, and the song of the milk-maid at her pail: and it is a sign of their being perverted, when they engender melancholy notions; for these are the off-spring of bigotry, fanaticism, and ignorance. The service of the Omnipotent is not of this gloomy cast; he has spread out the table of this beautiful world of wonders, for the use of his creatures, and has placed man at the head of it, that he might enjoy its bounties, as well as prepare himself for the approaching change to another, which inspiration has powerfully impressed on his soul as the *unknowable* region of his next ad-vance. The materialist, in his dreary reveries, can-not comprehend this, neither will he acknowledge that his being placed here is equally as miraculous as that

he should be placed in another world or worlds, pro-
gressively to improve, to all eternity : but to harbour
doubts on this subject, is like disputing the wisdom,
the justice, and the mercy of the Author of our being,
who, according to the conceptions we form of his
goodness, as exhibited in the design, the grandeur, and
the immensity of creation, where every thing is systema-
tic, regular, and in order, would never decree that man
should be placed here instinctively to know his Maker
—to take a short peep at the stupendous, the amazing
whole—to view all these, and have powers of mind
given him only to know and repugnantly to feel, that
after a life mixed with turmoil, grief, and disease, he is
to be annihilated ! In our conception of things, and to
the limited understanding which has been given us, all
this would appear to be labour in vain.

The volume of the creation speaks alike to all, and
cannot be defaced by man ; but the ways of Providence
are beyond his comprehension. Omnipotence has not
been pleased to gratify his pride and vanity, nor to
consult his understanding, in the government of the
universe; but sufficient has been disclosed unto him to
point out the moral duties he owes to society, and the
religious worship due to his Maker, without groping
after what is utterly beyond his reach: for our feeble
reason is too weak to comprehend the divine essence;
and our thoughts, on their utmost stretch, roll back

on darkness. We reason, but we err: for how can we comprehend the immensity of endless space, of time and eternity, a beginning or an end; or what conceptions can we form of the Power which made the sun and worlds without number? Truly, this is far too much for a finite being, who does not know why he can move one of his own fingers, or cease to do so when he pleases! But all may know and fulfil their religious obligations, by reverencing and adoring their Creator, and walking humbly before him, and their moral duties, by being in their several stations, good sons, brothers, husbands, wives, fathers, mothers, neighbours, and members of society.

Having, with humble diffidence, in this masquerade of life, attempted to point out to youth the exterior of the temple of virtue, and to lead them to its steps, the Editor leaves them there, respectfully recommending them to explore the whole interior, under the guidance of men more eminent for their mental powers and attainments in learning, philosophy, and piety. Of these, an illustrious band have placed, at every avenue and turning, their inestimable works, as directions to guide us to usefulness and respectability here, and eternal happiness hereafter.

Thomas Bewick

Newcastle, September, 1818.

THE INTRODUCTION.

FROM time to time, in all ages, men inspired, or gifted with a superior degree of intellectual power, have appeared upon the stage of life, in order (by enlightening others) to fulfil the designs of Omnipotence, in uniting the world in a state of civilized society.

Patriarchs, or heads of families, at first directed or governed those who were immediately dependent upon them: these in time increased, and became *clans;* these again, by their quarrels, and their wars, were induced to elect chieftains or kings over a number of united clans,—from which were formed the various nations and kingdoms of the earth.   In this early stage of the

b

world, when men were ignorant and uncivilized, the chase and war seem almost wholly to have occupied their time and attention. Their kings ruled over them with despotic sway, and the will of the prince was the only law: and thus the barbarism of the subject and the tyranny of the ruler went hand in hand together. That over-swollen pride, which seems the natural accompaniment of despotic power, blinds the understandings of its possessors, and renders them wholly regardless of the important trust reposed in them. The evils arising out of their bad government, are felt, more or less, by the whole people over whom they preside; and pride and arrogance prevent the approach of sincerity and truth. The sycophant and the slave then only find admission, and all other men are kept at a distance. While kings and governors were of this character, the voice of truth could only reach their ears through allegory and fable, which took their rise in the infancy of learning, and seem to have been the only safe mode of conveying admonition to tyrants. This pleasing method of instilling instruction into the mind, has been found by experience to be the shortest and best way of accomplishing that end, among all ranks and conditions of men.

The first Fable upon record, is that of Jotham and the Trees, in the Bible; and the next, that of The Poor Man and his Lamb, as related by Nathan to King David, and which carried with it a blaze of truth that flashed conviction on the mind of the royal transgressor. Lessons of reproof, religion, and morality, were, we find, continually delivered in this mode, by the sages of old, to the exalted among mankind.

It is asserted by authors, that Apologues and Fables had their origin in the Eastern world, and that the most ancient of them were the productions of Veeshnou Sarma, commonly called Pilpay, whose beautiful collections of Apologues were esteemed as sacred books in India and Persia, whence they were spread abroad among other nations, and were by them celebrated and holden in much estimation. They were translated from the Persian and Arabian into Greek, by Simeon Seth, a man of great learning, who was an officer of the imperial household at Constantinople about the year 1070. Seth's Version was imitated in Latin by Piers Alfonse, a converted Jew, as early as the year 1107; and this is supposed to have been the first version of Pilpay's Apologues that made its way, and became familiarized in Europe. The time in which Pilpay lived, seems not to be certainly known to the learned; but some of them suppose that the Fables of Æsop and others were grounded upon his models. The time in which Æsop lived is better ascertained, and of all the Fabulists who have amused and instructed mankind by their writings, his name stands pre-eminent. Authors fix his birth-place at Cotieum, in Phrygia Major. But the history of this remarkable person, who lived about 572 years before Christ, and about 100 years before Herodotus, the Greek historian, has been so involved in mystery, traditionary stories, and absurd conjectures, that any attempt to give a detail from such materials, would only serve to bewilder youth, and lead them into a labyrinth of error; and it would be impertinent to trouble the learned reader with that which must be sufficiently familiar to him.* The whole of the absurd fictions concerning this wise and amiable man, were invented by Maximus Planudes, a Greek monk.† Plutarch, and other authentic historians,‡ have, however, given a very different account of the illustrious Fabulist. It would appear, according to some of these relations, that Æsop, originally a shepherd's boy, had risen from the condition of a slave, to great eminence, and that he lived in the service of Xanthus and Judman, or Idmon, in the island of Samos, and afterwards at Athens. Phædrus speaks of him as living the greater part of his life at the latter place, where, it appears, a handsome statue, executed by the hand of the famous statuary Lysippus, was erected to his memory, and placed before those of the seven sages of Greece.§ He also notices his living at Samos, and interesting himself in a public capacity, in the administration of the affairs of that place; where Aristotle also introduces him as a public speaker, and records the fact of his reciting the fable of the Fox and the Hedgehog,¶ while pleading on behalf of a minister, upon the occasion of his being impeached for embezzling the

* The curious enquirer is referred to the Essay on the Æsopean Fable, by Sir Brooke Boothby, bart. from which this sketch is extracted.

† Planudes lived at Constantinople in the 14th century. His Fables were printed at Milan, A. D. 1480.

‡ The first person who took great pains to detect and expose the follies and absurdities of Planudes's Life of Æsop, and collected what could be known, was Bachet de Mezeriac, a man of great learning, who flourished about the year 1632.

§ These sages were Solon, Thales, Chilo, Cleobulus, Bias, Pittacus, and Periander, to whom Laertius adds Anacharsis, Maro, Pherecydes, Epimenides, and Pisistratus.

¶ " Ye men of Samos, let me entreat you to do as the Fox did; for this man, having got money enough, can have no further occasion to rob public treasure. Æsop is also mentioned as speaking in a public capacity to the Athenians, at the time when Pisistratus seized upon their liberties.* Upon each of these occasions he is represented as having introduced a Fable into his discourse, in a witty and pleasing manner. He was holden in the highest veneration and esteem in his day, by all men eminent for their wisdom and virtue. It appears there was scarcely an author among the ancient Greeks who mixed any thing of morality in his writings, that did not either quote or mention Æsop. Plato describes Socrates as turning some of Æsop's Fables into verse, during those awful hours which he spent in prison, immediately before his death. Aristophanes not only takes hints from Æsop, but mentions him much to his honour, as one whose works were, or ought to be, read before any other. Ennius and Horace have embellished their poetry from his stores; and ancient sages and authors all concur in bearing the most ample testimony to his distinguished merits. Plutarch, in his imaginary banquet of the seven wise men, among several other illustrious persons of ancient times, celebrated for their wit and knowledge, introduces Æsop, and describes him as being very courtly and polite in his behaviour. Upon the authority of Plutarch also, we fix the life of Æsop in the time of Crœsus, king of Lydia, who invited him to the court of Sardis. By this prince, he was holden in such

you; but if you put him to death, some needy person will fill his place, whose wants must be supplied out of your property."

The Fable of the Fox and the Hedge-hog was applied by Themistocles to dissuade the Athenians from removing their magistrates.— *B. Boothby.*

* The Fable of the Frogs desiring a King.

esteem, as to be sent as his envoy to Periander, king of Corinth, which was about three hundred and twenty years after the time in which Homer lived, and 550 before Christ. He was also deputed by Crœsus to consult the oracle of Delphi. While on this embassy, he was ordered to distribute to each of the citizens, four *minæ** of silver, but some disputes arising between them and Æsop, he reproached them for their indolence, in suffering their lands to lie uncultivated, and in depending on the gratuities of strangers for a precarious subsistence: the quarrel, which it would appear ran high between them, ended in Æsop's sending back the money to Sardis. This so exasperated the Delphians, that they resolved upon his destruction; and that they might have some colour of justice for what they intended, they concealed among his effects, when he was taking his departure from Delphi, a gold cup, consecrated to Apollo; and afterwards pursuing him, easily found what they themselves had hidden. On the pretext that he had committed this sacrilegious theft, they carried him back to the city, and notwithstanding his imprecating upon them the vengeance of heaven, they immediately condemned him to be cast from the rock Hypania, as the punishment of the pretended crime. Ancient historians say, that for this wickedness, the Delphians were for a long time visited with pestilence and famine, until an expiation was made, and then the plague ceased.

It was not until many ages after the death of Æsop, that his most prominent successor, Phædrus, arose. He

---

* The mina of silver was 12 ounces, about £3 sterling.

translated Æsop's Fables from the Greek into Latin, and added to them many of his own. Of Phædrus little is known, except from his works. He is said to have lived in the times of the Emperors Augustus and Tiberius, and to have died in the reign of the latter. The first printed edition of his Fables, with cuts, was published at Gauda, in 1482. Caxton published some of them in 1484, and Bonus Accursius in 1489, to which he prefixed Planudes's Life of Æsop. But the most perfect edition of Phædrus's Works was published in five volumes, by Peter Pithou, at Troyes, in 1596, from manuscripts discovered by him in the cities of Rheims and Dijon. To these have succeeded in later times, a numerous list of fabulists,* besides such of the poets as have occasionally interspersed Fables in their works. These, in their day, have had, and many of them still have, their several admirers; but Gay and Dodsley best maintain their ground in this country, as is proved by the regular demand for new editions. Croxall's Fables, which were first published in 1722, with cuts on metal, in the manner of wood, have also had a most extensive sale; and Sir Brooke Boothby's

---

* Sir Roger L'Estrange, born 1616, died 1704.

John de la Fontaine, born 1621, died 1695.

John Dryden, born 1631, died 1701.

Antoine Houdart de la Motte, born 1672, died 1731.

John Gay, born 1688, died 1732.

Samuel Croxall, D. D. Archdeacon of Hereford, died 1752.

Edward Moore, died 1757.

Draper.

Robert Dodsley, born 1703, died 1764.

William Wilkie, born 1721, died 1772.

Abbe Brotier, born 1722, died 1789.

elegant little volumes, in verse, published in 1809, are now making their way into the public notice. The Editor of the present volume, in attempting to continue the same pleasing mode of conveying instruction, long since laid down as a guide to virtue, has quoted and compiled from other fabulists, whatever seemed best suited to his purpose. His sole object is utility, and he is not altogether without hope, that in attempting to embellish and perpetuate a fabric, which has its foundations laid in religion and morality, his efforts may not be wholly ineffectual to induce the young to keep steadily in view those great truths, which form the sure land-mark to the haven, where only they can attain peace and happiness.

THE TABLE OF CONTENTS.

A

c

B

C

D

xxiii

P

R

S

T

THE

FABLES OF ÆSOP,

AND OTHERS.

THE TWO CRABS.

Two Crabs, the mother and daughter, having been left
by the receding tide, were creeping again towards the
water, when the former observing the awkward gait of
her daughter, got into a great passion, and desired her
to move straight forward, in a more becoming and
sprightly manner, and not crawl sideling along in a way
so contrary to all the rest of the world. Indeed mother,
says the young Crab, I walk as properly as I can, and
to the best of my knowledge; but if you would have

B

me to go otherwise, I beg you would be so good as to practise it first, and shew me by your own example how you would have me to conduct myself.

APPLICATION.

ILL examples corrupt even the best natural disposi-tion, and it is in vain to instruct our children, their talents being only imitation, to walk by one rule, if we ourselves go by another. The good precepts which we may lay down to them, will be bestowed in vain, if they see by our own conduct, that we pursue a contrary course to that which we recommend to them. Parents therefore, who are desirous of working an effectual re-formation in their children, should begin by making a visible amendment in themselves; and this is a duty they owe to society, as well as to their offspring, it be-ing of the utmost importance to both, that probity and honour be early instilled into their youthful minds, as these grow with their growth, and while at the same time they command respect, they lay the foundation of their individual happiness through life.

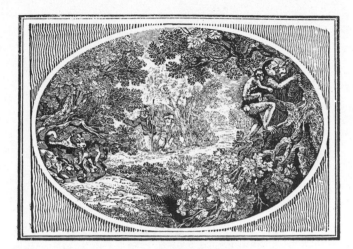

THE APE AND HER YOUNG ONES.

An Ape having two young ones, was dotingly fond of one, but disregarded and slighted the other. One day she chanced to be surprized by the hunters, and had much ado to get off. However, she did not forget her favourite young one, which she took up in her arms, that it might be the more secure : the other, which she neglected, by natural instinct, leapt upon her back, and so away they scampered together; but it unluckily fell out, in the over-anxiety of her precipitate flight, confused and blinded with haste, that she struck her favourite's head against a branch, which threw it on the ground, where the darling bantling was seized by the dogs and killed. The hated one, clinging close to her rough back, escaped all the danger of the pursuit.

APPLICATION.

By dear mamma's o'er-weening fondness spoil'd,
Caress'd and pamper'd, dies the fav'rite child:
The boy she slights, rough, vig'rous, and well-grown,
Unaided, bears the brunt, and shifts alone.

THE indulgence which parents shew to their children arises from the most amiable of human weaknesses; but it is not the less injurious in its effects, and therefore it is of great importance to guard against it, and not to suffer a blind fondness to transport us beyond the bounds of a discreet affection, for this often proves the ruin of the child. This fable is also intended to expose the folly of a system of favouritism in families, for experience shews that those children who are the least pampered and indulged usually make the best and cleverest men.

THE BOY AND HIS MOTHER.

A little Boy having stolen a book from one of his school-fellows, took it to his Mother, who, instead of correcting him, praised his sharpness, and rewarded him. In process of time, as he grew bigger, he increased also in villainy, till at length he was taken up for committing a great robbery, and was brought to justice and condemned for it. As the officers were conducting him to the gallows, he was attended by a vast crowd, and among the rest his Mother came sobbing along, and deploring her son's unhappy fate; which the criminal observing, he begged leave to speak to her: this being granted, he put his mouth to her ear, as if he was going to whisper something, and bit it off! The officer, shocked at this behaviour, asked him if the crimes he had committed were not sufficient to glut his wickedness, without being also guilty of such an unnatural violence towards his mother? Let no one wonder, said he, that I have done this to her, for she deserves even worse at my hands. For if she had chastised instead of praising and encouraging me, when I stole my school-fellow's book, I should not now have been brought to this ignominious and untimely end.

APPLICATION.

THE approaches to vice are by slow degrees, and the good or evil bias given to youth is seldom eradicated. The first deviations from sound morality should therefore be most strictly watched, and wickedness checked or punished in time; for when vice grows into a habit, it becomes incurable, and both good governments and private families are deeply concerned in its attendant consequences. One need not scruple to affirm that most of the depravity which is so frequent in the world, and so pernicious to society, is owing to the bad education of youth; and to the connivance or ill example of their parents. It is therefore of the utmost consequence that parents, guardians, and tutors, should be of characters befitting them for the various and important offices they have to perform. The latter description of persons may and ought to be carefully selected; but it is to be lamented that the base and mean-spirited hosts of bad parents are out of the reach of controul, and nothing can prevent the evils arising from their tutorage. Perhaps it would be harsh to make laws to check the marriages of such; but there is no need to encourage the breed of them, for they are already over abundantly numerous.

THE MASTER AND HIS SCHOLAR.

As a School-master was walking upon the bank of a river, he heard a cry as of one in distress: advancing a few paces farther, he saw one of his Scholars in the water, hanging by the branch of a willow. The Boy had, it seems, been learning to swim with corks, and now thinking himself sufficiently experienced, had thrown these implements aside, and ventured into the water without them; but the force of the stream having hurried him out of his depth, he had certainly been drowned, had not the branch of the tree providentially hung in his way. The Master took up the corks, which lay upon the ground, and throwing them to his Scholar, made use of this opportunity to read a lecture to him upon the inconsiderate rashness of youth. Let this be an example to you, says he, in the conduct of your future life, never to throw away your corks till time has given you strength and experience enough to swim without them.

RASHNESS is the peculiar vice of youth, and may be stiled the characteristic foible of that season of life. The foundation of this rashness is laid in a fond conceit of their own abilities, which tempts them to undertake affairs too great for their capacities, and to venture out of their depths, or to suffer themselves to be hurried into the most precipitate and dangerous measures, before they find out their own weakness and inability. It therefore behoves inexperienced young men to keep a cautious guard over their passions, to check the irregularities of their disposition, and to listen to the wholesome advice and good council of those whose judgments are matured by age and experience: for few are above the need of advice, nor are we ever too old to learn any thing for which we may be the better. But young men, above all, should not disdain to open their eyes to good example, and their ears to admonition : neither should they be ashamed to borrow rules for their behaviour in the world, until they are enabled from their own knowledge of men and things, to stem its crooked tides and currents with ease and honour to themselves.

> Consult your elders, use their sense alone,
> Till age and practice have confirm'd your own.

INDUSTRY AND SLOTH.

AN indolent Young Man being asked why he lay in bed so long? jocosely answered, " Every morning of my life I am hearing causes. I have two fine girls, their names are Industry and Sloth, close at my bed-side as soon as I awake, pressing their different suits. One intreats me to get up, the other persuades me to lie still; and then they alternately give me various reasons why I should rise, and why I should not. This detains me so long, (it being the duty of an impartial judge to hear all that can be said on either side) that before the pleadings are over, it is time to go to dinner."

c

APPLICATION.

" He who defers his work from day to day,
Does on a river's brink expecting stay,
'Till the whole stream which stopt him shall be gone,
Which, as it runs, for ever will run on."

INDOLENCE is like a stream which flows slowly on, but
yet it undermines every virtue; it rusts the mind, and
gives a tincture to every action of one's life, the term of
which does not allow time for long protracted delibera-
tions; and yet how many waste more of their time in
idly considering which of two affairs to begin first, than
would have ended them both? To-morrow is still the
fatal time when all is to be done; to-morrow comes, it
goes, and still indolence pleases itself with the shadow,
while it loses the substance: and thus men pass through
life like a bird through the air, and leave no track behind them, unmindful that the present time alone is
ours, and should be managed with judicious care, since
we cannot secure a moment to come, nor recal one
that is past. It is no matter how many good qualities
the mind may be possessed of; they all lie dormant if
we want the necessary vigour and resolution to draw
them forth; for this slumber of the mind leaves no difference between the greatest genius and the meanest
understanding. Neither the mind nor the body can be
active and vigorous without proper exertion, and trouble springs from idleness, and grievous toil from useless
ease; therefore, " whatsoever thy hand findeth to do,
do it with all thy might, for there is no work, nor device, nor knowledge, nor wisdom in the grave, whither
thou goest."

THE YOUNG MAN AND THE SWALLOW.

A prodigal thoughtless young Man, who had wasted his whole patrimony in taverns and gaming-houses, among his lewd idle companions, was taking a melancholy walk near a brook. It was in the spring, while the hills were yet capped with snow, but it happened to be one of those clear sunny days which some times occur at that time of the year; and to make appearances the more flattering, a Swallow which had been invited forth by the warmth, flew skimming along upon the surface of the water. The Youth observing this, concluded that the summer was now come, and that he should have little or no occasion for clothes, so went and pawned them, and ventured the money for one stake more, among his sharping associates. When this too was gone, like all the rest of his property, he took another solitary walk in the same place as before, but the weather being severe and frosty, every thing had put on a very different aspect; the brook was frozen over, and the poor Swallow lay dead upon the bank. At this, the Youth, smarting under the sense of his own misery, mistakingly reproached the Swallow as the cause of all his misfortunes: he cried out, oh, unhappy bird, thou hast undone both thyself and me, who was so credulous as to trust to thy appearance.

APPLICATION.

THEY who frequent taverns and gaming-houses, and keep bad company, should not wonder if they are reduced in a very short time to penury and want. The wretched young fellows who once addict themselves to such a scandalous course of life, scarcely think of or attend to any thing besides: they seem to have nothing else in their heads but how they may squander what they have got, and where they may get more when that is gone. They do not make the same use of their reason as other people, but like the jaundiced eye, view every thing in a false light, and having turned a deaf ear to all advice, and pursued their unaltered course until all their property is irrecoverably lost, when at length misery forces upon them a sense of their situation, they still lay the blame upon any cause but the right one—their own extravagance and folly; like the Prodigal in the fable, who would not have considered a solitary occurrence as a general indication of the season, had not his own wicked desires blinded his understanding.

THE COLLIER AND THE FULLER.

THE Collier and the Fuller being old acquaintances, happened upon a time to meet together, and the latter being but ill provided with a habitation, was invited by the former to come and live in the same house with him. I thank you, my dear friend, replied the Fuller, for your kind offer; but it cannot be, for if I were to dwell with you, whatever I should take pains to scour and make clean in the morning, the dust of you and your coals would blacken and defile before night.

APPLICATION.

IT is of no small importance in life to be cautious what company we keep, and with whom we enter into friendship; for though we are ever so well disposed ourselves, and free from vice, yet if those with whom

we frequently converse, are engaged in a lewd, wicked
course, it will be almost impossible for us to escape
being drawn in with them.   If we are truly wise, and
would shun those rocks of pleasure upon which so many
have split, we should forbid ourselves all manner of
commerce and correspondence with those who are steer-
ing a course, which reason tells us is not only not for
our advantage, but would end in our destruction.   All
the virtue we can boast of, will not be sufficient to insure our safety, if we embark in bad company; for
though our philosophy were such as would preserve us
from being tainted and infected with their manners, yet
their characters would twist and entwine themselves
along with ours, in so intricate a fold, that the world
would not take the trouble to unravel and separate
them.   Reputation is of a blending nature, like water;
that which is derived from the clearest spring, if it
chance to mix with a foul current, runs on undistin-
guished, in one muddy stream, and must ever partake
of the colour and condition of its associate.

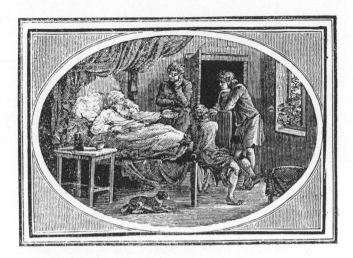

THE HUSBANDMAN AND HIS SONS.

A HUSBANDMAN, at the point of death, being desirous that his Sons should pursue the same innocent
course of agriculture in which he himself had been engaged all his life, made use of this expedient. He
called them to his bed-side, and said: All the patrimony I have to bequeath to you, my sons, is my farm
and my vine-yard, of which I make you joint heirs;
but I charge you not to let them go out of your own
occupation, for if I have any treasure besides, it lies
buried somewhere in the ground within a foot of the
surface. This made the Sons conclude that he talked of
money which he had hidden: so after their father's
death, with unwearied diligence, they carefully dug up
every inch, and though they found not the money they
expected, the ground, by being well stirred and loosen-
ed, produced so plentiful a crop of all that was sown in
it, as proved a real, and that no inconsiderable treasure.

APPLICATION.

THE good name and the good counsel of a father, are the best legacies he can leave to his children; and they ought to revere the one, and keep in mind the other. The wealth which a man acquires by his honest industry affords him greater pleasure in the enjoyment, than when acquired in any other way; and men who by personal labour have obtained a competency, know its value better than those can who have had it showered upon them without any efforts of their own. Idleness engenders disease, while exercise is the great prop of health, and health is the greatest blessing of life, which consideration alone ought to stimulate men to pursue some useful employment; and among the almost endless number of those, to which good laws and well-organized society give birth and encouragement, there are none equal to the culture of the earth, none which yield a more grateful return. The pleasures derived both from agriculture and horticulture, are so various, so delightful, and so natural to man, that they are not easily to be described, and are never to be excelled: for in whatever way they are pursued, the mind may be constantly entertained with the wonderful œconomy of the vegetable world; and the nerves are invigorated and kept in proper tone by the freshness of the earth, and the fragrancy of the air, which blush the countenance with health, and give a relish to every meal.

THE PROUD FROG AND THE OX.

An Ox, grazing in a meadow, chanced to set his foot among a parcel of young Frogs, and trod one of them to death. The rest informed their mother, when she came home, what had happened; telling her, that the beast which did it, was the hugest creature that they ever saw in their lives. What, was it so big? says the old Frog, swelling and blowing up her speckled belly to a great degree. Oh! bigger by a vast deal, say they: and so big? says she, straining herself yet more. Indeed, say they, if you were to burst yourself, you would never be so big. She strove yet again, and burst herself indeed.

D

APPLICATION.

How many vain people, of moderate easy circumstances, by entertaining the silly ambition of vying with
their superiors in station and fortune, get into the direct
road to ruin.   In whatever station of life it may have
pleased Providence to place us, we ought to determine
upon living within our income, and to endeavour by
honesty, sobriety, and industry, to maintain our ground.
Young men, upon their launching out into the world,
would do well deeply to reflect upon this, for their future peace of mind and happiness greatly depend upon
it.   They need only look a little about them to see
how a contrary conduct has operated upon thousands;
and it is to be feared, will continue to fill our gaols with
debtors, and Bedlam with lunatics.

THE STAG LOOKING INTO THE WATER.

A Stag drinking, saw himself in the water, and pleased with the sight, stood contemplating his shape. Ah, says he, what a glorious pair of branching horns are here, how gracefully do these antlers project over my forehead, and give an agreeable turn to my whole face; but I have such legs as really make me ashamed; they look so very long and unsightly, that I had rather have none at all. In the midst of this soliloquy, he was alarmed with the cry of a pack of hounds. Away he flies in some consternation, and bounding nimbly over the plain, threw dogs and men at a vast distance behind him. After which, taking a very thick copse, he had the ill fortune to be entangled by his horns in the branches, where he was held fast till the hounds came up and seized him. In the pangs of death, he is said to have uttered these words: Unhappy creature that I am, I am too late convinced that what I prided myself in, has been the cause of my undoing; and what I so much disliked, was the only thing that could have saved me.

APPLICATION.

WE often make a false estimate, in preferring our ornamental talents to our useful ones, and are apt to place our love and admiration on wrong objects. When our vanity is stronger than our reason, show and ostentation find easy admission into our hearts, and we are much fonder of specious trifles than useful plainness. But the truest mark of wisdom is to estimate things at their just value, and to know whence the most solid advantages may be derived: otherwise, like the Stag in the Fable, we may happen to admire those accomplishments which are not only of no real use, but often prove prejudicial to us, while we despise those things on which our safety may depend. He that does not know himself, will often form a false judgment upon other matters that most materially concern him; and thus it fares with many, who suffer themselves to be deluded with the false pomp of high life, and whose vanity prompts them to conceive they possess talents which qualify them to shine in that circle, into which, had they judged rightly, they never would have entered, but rather have applied themselves to improve other qualifications, which might have insured their own happiness, and have rendered them useful members of society.

THE LEOPARD AND THE FOX.

THE Leopard, one day, took it into his head to value himself upon the great variety and beauty of his spots, and truly he saw no reason why even the Lion should take place of him, since he could not shew so beautiful a skin. As for the rest of the wild beasts of the forest, he treated them all without distinction in the most haughty and disdainful manner. But the Fox being among them, went up to him with a great deal of spirit and resolution, and told him that he was mistaken in the value he was pleased to set upon himself, since people of judgment were not used to form their opinion of merit from an outside appearance, but by considering the good qualities and endowments with which the mind was stored within.

APPLICATION.

WISE men are chiefly captivated with the beauty of the mind, rather than that of the person; and whenever they are infatuated with a passion for any thing else, it is generally observed that they cease, during that time at least, to be what they were, and indeed are only considered to be playing the fool. It too often happens that women of remarkable beauty are so fully satisfied with their outward excellencies, that they totally neglect the improvement of their minds; not considering that it is only a combination of mental and personal charms that can entitle them to be ranked as Nature's greatest ornaments. Unmindful of this, however, they are too apt to consider beauty as the only thing requisite in their sex; and since they are endowed with it in such an eminent degree, they look down with disdain on females less happy in personal charms. Beauty has undoubtedly great influence over the hearts of mankind, but when it is overrun with affectation and conceit, their admiration will soon be turned into disgust; while women of more ordinary persons, but blessed with good sense and good humour, will captivate the hearts of worthy men, and more effectually secure their constancy.

THE PEACOCK AND THE CRANE.

THE Peacock and the Crane having by chance met together, the Peacock erected his tail, displayed his gaudy plumes, and looked with contempt upon the Crane, as some mean ordinary person. The Crane resolving to mortify his insolence, took occasion to say, that Peacocks were very fine birds indeed, if fine feathers could make them so; but that he thought it a much nobler thing to be able to rise above the clouds into endless space, and survey the wonders of the heavens, as well as of the earth beneath, with its seas, lakes, and rivers, as far as the eye can reach, than to strut about upon the ground, and be gazed at by children.

APPLICATION.

THERE cannot be a greater sign of a weak mind,

than a person's valuing himself on a gaudy outside, whether it consist of the beauties of the person, or the still more contemptible vanity of fine cloaths. This kind of misguided pride, while it endeavours to exalt, commonly tends to lower the persons who are infected with it; but never renders them so truly ridiculous as when it inspires them with a contempt of those who have ten times more worth than themselves. To value ourselves upon the glitter and finery of dress is one of the most trifling of all vanities; and a man of sense would be ashamed to bestow upon it the least attention. They who examine things by the scale of common sense, must find something of weight and substance before they can be persuaded to set a value upon it. The mind that is stored with virtuous and rational sentiments, and the behaviour which is founded upon complacency and humility, stamp a value upon the possessor, which all men of discernment are ever ready to admire and acknowledge.

THE TWO POTS.

An earthen Pot, and one of brass, standing together upon the brink of a river, were both carried away by the sudden rise of the water. The earthen Pot shewed some uneasiness, fearing he should be broken; but his companion of brass bade him be under no apprehension, as he would take care of him. Oh! replies the other, keep as far off as you can, I entreat you: it is you I am most afraid of; for whether the stream dash you against me, or me against you, I am sure to be the sufferer, and, therefore, I beg of you do not let us come near one another.

APPLICATION.

A man of moderate fortune, who is contented with what he has, and finds he can live happily upon it,

E

should be particularly guarded against the ill-judged ambition of associating with the rich and powerful, for what in them is œconomy, would in him be the height of extravagance; and at the very time they honour him with their countenance, they are leading him on to his ruin. People of equal conditions may float down the current of life without hurting each other; but it is no easy matter to steer one's course in company with the great, so as to escape without a bulge: neither is it desirable to live in the neighbourhood of a very great man; for whether we ignorantly trespass upon him, or he knowingly encroach upon us, we are sure to be the sufferers.

THE MOLE AND HER DAM.

THE young Mole snuffed up her nose, and told her Dam she smelt an odd kind of a smell. Bye and bye, O strange! says she, what a noise there is in my ears, as if ten thousand hammers were going. A little after, she was at it again: look, look, what is that I see yonder? it is just like the flame of a fiery furnace. The Dam replied, pray child hold your idle tongue; and if you would have us allow you any sense at all, do not affect to shew more than nature has given you.

APPLICATION.

BY affectation, we aim at being thought to possess some accomplishment which we have not, or at shewing what we have, in a conceited ostentatious manner. There is scarcely any species of ridiculous behaviour, which is not derived from it; it grows out of folly and insincerity; it derogates from genius; it is the bane of beauty, and diminishes its charms; it is disagreeable to others, and hurtful to the person who uses it; it detracts from some real possession, and makes qualities that would otherwise pass well enough, appear nauseous and offensive; and whoever indulges in it, may be sure to lay themselves open, and call forth the attention of others to notice their vanity. To cure ourselves of affectation, we have only to call in the aids of truth and sincerity, which will cut off the whole train of its follies at one stroke.

THE GOAT, THE KID, AND THE WOLF.

THE Goat going abroad to feed, shut up her young Kid at home, charging him to bolt the door fast, and open it to nobody till she herself should return. The Wolf who lay lurking hard by, heard the charge given, and soon after came and knocked at the door, counterfeiting the voice of the Goat, and desired to be admitted. The Kid looking out at the window, and finding the cheat, bade him go about his business, for, however he might imitate a Goat's voice, yet he appeared too much like a Wolf to be trusted.

APPLICATION.

DECEIT, hypocrisy, and villainy, are constantly on the watch to entrap and ensnare the innocent and the unwary. Every beautiful woman is commonly sur-

rounded by a kind of men who would undermine her
virtue; and inexperienced men of fortune, in the outset of life, are almost constantly beset with rogues and
sharpers; and these artful villains, under one specious
pretext or another, too often effect the ruin of the
weak and unsuspicious of both sexes.   As a guard
against all these, the early admonitions of parents are
of inestimable worth : they are built upon the tenderest
regard, and the most sincere affection.   Those who
have already travelled over the difficult paths of life,
and buffeted its storms, have observed the snares and
the dangers with which the way is strewed, and they are
enabled by their experience, to forewarn those who are
about to launch out on the troubled ocean of life, to
steer their course clear of its hidden rocks, its shoals,
and its quick-sands.   Did youth but know the importance of this early advice, how eagerly would they
treasure it in their minds, and as occasion required,
with what pleasure would they draw it forth, and obey
its dictates.   To the neglect of these precepts, may be
attributed much of the ill conduct we see in the world,
and most of the misfortunes which befal mankind
through life.

THE BROTHER AND SISTER.

A certain man had two children, a Son and a Daughter; the Boy very handsome, and the Girl only moderately so. They were both young, and happened to be one day playing near the looking-glass, which stood on their mother's toilet. The Boy, pleased with the novelty of the thing, viewed himself for some time, and in a wanton roguish manner, observed to the Girl how handsome he was. She resented it, and could not bear the insolent manner in which he spoke, for she understood it (as how could she do otherwise) to be intended as a direct affront to her. Therefore she ran immediately to her Father, and with a deal of aggravation, complained of her Brother, particularly of his having acted so effeminate a part as to look in a glass, and meddle with things which belonged to women only. The father embraced them both with much tenderness and affection, and told them that he should like to have them look in a glass every day : to the intent that you, says he, addressing himself to the Boy, if you think that face of yours handsome, may not disgrace and spoil it by an ugly temper, and a foul behaviour; and that you, speaking to the girl, may make up for the defects of your person, if there be any, by the sweetness of your manners, and the agreeableness of your conversation.

APPLICATION.

WE should every day view ourselves considerately in a looking-glass, with the intent of converting it to a better purpose than that of merely observing and admiring our persons. Let those on whom nature has been liberal of her bounties, in bestowing a fine countenance, with symmetry of person, health, and strength, always remember that these are the gifts of providence, for which we ought ever to be thankful, but never vain : these qualifications ought only to act as a spur to induce us to cultivate the mind, by study, by reading, and reflection, so as to cause it to correspond in its beauties with those of our outward appearance. Let others again who have not any thing in their personal appearance to attract the attention of the world, strive also to improve the faculties of the mind, and to excel in the beauties of a good temper, and an agreeable conversation, the charms of which, notwithstanding a rough exterior, cannot fail to endear the possessor to all men of sense, who will readily discover intrinsic worth, whether it be made up of a lively imagination, clear perceptions, or the transparent sincerity of an honest heart.

THE SHEEP-BITER.

A certain Shepherd had a Dog, upon whose fidelity he relied very much, for whenever he had occasion to be absent himself, he committed the care of his flock to the charge of this Dog; and to encourage him to do his duty cheerfully, he fed him constantly with sweet milk and curds, and sometimes threw him a bone extraordinary. Yet, notwithstanding this, no sooner was his back turned, than the treacherous Cur fell upon some one of the flock, and thus devoured the sheep instead of guarding and defending them. The Shepherd having at length found out his tricks, was resolved to hang him; and the Dog, when the rope was about his neck, and he was just going to be tied up, began to expostulate with his master, asking him why he was so unmercifully bent against him, who was his own servant and creature, and had only committed a few crimes;

F

and why he did not rather take vengeance on the Wolf
who was an open and declared enemy? Nay, replied
the Shepherd, it is for that very reason that I think
you ten times more worthy of death, for from him I
expected nothing but hostilities, and therefore could
guard against him; you I depended on as a just and
faithful servant, and fed and encouraged you accordingly, and therefore your treachery is the more base,
and your ungratitude the more unpardonable.

APPLICATION.

THE common disappointments which we are liable
to through life, do not bring with them any thing to
be compared to the bitterness we experience from the
perfidy of those we esteemed and trusted as friends : an
open enemy we can guard against, and we look upon
him when he is at rest, as we do at the sword within its
scabbard; but the man who betrays his trust, masked
under the appearance of friendship, wounds us in the
tenderest part, and involves us in a cruelly complicated
grief, which frets the mind and heightens the sum of
our infelicity. Friendship is the cordial of human life,
the balm of society; and he who violates its laws, by
treachery and deceit, converts it into the deadliest
poison, and renders that which ought to be the defence and support of our steps, our greatest snare and
danger.

THE OLD WOMAN AND HER MAIDS.

An Old Woman, who had several Maid Servants,
used to call them up to their work at the crowing of the
Cock. The damsels, not liking to have their sweet
slumbers disturbed so early, combined together, and
killed the Cock, thinking they might then enjoy their
warm beds a little longer. But in this they found
themselves mistaken, for the Old Woman, having lost
her unerring guide, from that time roused them out
of their beds whenever she awoke, although it might be
at midnight.

APPLICATION.

We govern our lives by imagination rather than by
judgment, mistaking the reason of things, and impu-
ting the issue of them to wrong causes. We should

endeavour to content ourselves in our present station, if it be not very bad indeed, for it seldom happens that every thing can be in all respects agreeable to our wishes. When we give full scope to the impatience of our tempers, and quit our present condition in life, we often find we have not changed for the better; but we are too fond of carving out our fortunes for ourselves, and wish to remove this or that obstacle which we imagine stands between us and our felicity: then, too late, we see how greatly we are mistaken in our notions, when we feel we have changed for the worse. Before we attempt any alteration of moment, we should, if possible, ascertain what state it will produce, and not suffer infirmity of temper to embitter our lives; but, above all, we should never aim at mending our fortunes by fraud and violence.

They all want Brains Wigs

HERCULES AND THE CARTER.

As a clownish Fellow was driving his cart along a deep miry lane, the wheels stuck so fast in the clay, that his horses could not draw it out. Upon this he fell a bawling and praying to Hercules to come and help him. Hercules, looking down from a cloud, bid him not lie there like an idle dastardly looby as he was, but get up and whip his horses, and clap his shoulder stoutly to the wheel, adding that this was the only way for him to obtain assistance.

APPLICATION.

THE man who sits down at his ease, and prays to Heaven to have all his wants supplied, and his wishes accomplished, by a miracle wrought in his favour, without using his own exertions and honest endeavours to obtain them, deserves to be disappointed. Many men who have a fair share of natural good sense, and who also value themselves upon having their reasoning powers enlightened by revelation, yet fall into this error: led by fanatics and bigots, they follow the fashion of running often to prayers and sermons, when they might be much better employed at home. The industrious good man, instead of publicly praying for the comforts of life, pursues his business, which is the proper means of procuring them; and if at the same time he holds converse with his Maker, which all men ought to do, and no man can be happy without doing, he needs no veil of hypocrisy to make the world believe he is better than he really is: he feels it his duty and pleasure so to proceed, while he sojourns here, and knows not how he can do better, than by sober and honest industry to provide for those of his own household, and to endeavour for the means of helping him that needeth. The man who is virtuously and honestly engaged, is actually serving God all the while; and is more likely to have his silent wishes, accompanied with strenuous endeavours, complied with by the Supreme Being, than he who begs with an unnecessary vehemence, and solicits with an empty hand—a hand which would be more religious, were it usefully employed, and more devout, were it stretched out to do good to those that want it.

THE EAGLE, THE CAT, AND THE SOW.

An Eagle had built her nest upon the top branches of an old oak; a Wild Cat inhabited a hole in the middle; and in the hollow part at the bottom was a Sow with a whole litter of Pigs. A happy neighbourhood, and might long have continued so, had it not been for the wicked insinuations of the designing Cat: for first of all, up she crept to the Eagle, and, Good neighbour, says she, we shall all be undone; that filthy Sow yonder does nothing but lie rooting at the foot of the tree, and, as I suspect, intends to grub it up, that she may the more easily come at our young ones. For my part, I will take care of my own concerns, you may do as you please; but I will watch her motions, though I stay at home this month for it. When she had said this, which could not fail of putting the Eagle into a great fright, down she went, and made a visit to the

Sow at the bottom: putting on a sorrowful face, I hope, says she, you do not intend to go abroad to-day: why not? says the Sow: nay, replies the other, you may do as you please, but I overheard the Eagle tell her young ones, that she would treat them with a Pig the first time she saw you go out; and I am not sure but she may take up with a Kitten in the mean time; so good morrow to you, you will excuse me, I must go and take care of the little folks at home. Away she went accordingly, and by contriving to steal out softly at nights for her prey, and to stand watching and peeping all day at her hole, as under great concern, she made such an impression upon the Eagle and the Sow, that neither of them dared to venture abroad, for fear of the other; the consequence of which was, that they in a little time were starved, and their young ones fell a prey to the treacherous Cat and her Kittens.

APPLICATION.

THIS shews us the ill consequence of giving ear to a gossiping double-tongued neighbour. Many sociable well-disposed families have been blown up into a perpetual discord, by one of these wicked go-betweens; so that whoever would avoid the imputation of being a bad neighbour, should guard both against receiving ill impressions by hearsay, and uttering his opinions of others, to those busy bodies, who, to gratify a malignant disposition, or gain some selfish end of their own, can magnify a gnat to the size of a camel, or swell a mole-hill to a mountain.

THE LARK AND HER YOUNG ONES.

A Lark who had Young Ones in a field of corn nearly ripe, was under some fear lest the reapers should come and cut it down before her young brood were fledged, and able to remove from the place; wherefore, when she flew abroad in the morning to seek for food for them, she charged them to listen to what the Farmer said about shearing.   On her return, her young family opened all their little throats at once, to inform her that the Farmer had sent to his neigh- bours to reap the corn the next morning.   Is that all? said the old Lark, then there is no danger.   When she went abroad again the next morning, she left the same instructions as before.   At night, she found her Young Ones more alarmed than at first; for the Farmer had applied to his friends, earnestly requesting them to begin the harvest the next day.   She received this

intelligence as calmly as before, and took no other
precautions the next day, than repeating the same orders.   In the evening, they told her that the Farmer
had been charging his son to get the sickles ready, for
it was in vain to wait for other people, and that they
would cut the corn to-morrow themselves.   Nay, then
said the old Lark, we must be off as soon as we can ; for
when a man undertakes to do his business himself, it is
not so likely that he will be disappointed.

APPLICATION.

He who depends on the assistance of others to perform what he is able to do himself, must not be surprised to find that his business is neglected.   He may
be sure that it will be best done when he puts forth his
own hands, and looks after it with his own eyes.   How
indeed can any man imagine, that other people will be
active in his interest, while he himself remains indolent
and unconcerned about his own affairs.   Men of such
tempers and dispositions, live in a state of suspense,
and subject themselves to perpetual disappointments
and losses, which their own industry would have pre-
vented, and have kept their minds at ease.   They do
not use their reasoning powers, but sink down into a
kind of stupid abject dependence upon others, which
degrades even the finest talents with which human
nature is dignified.

THE YOUNG MEN AND THE COOK.

Two Young Men went into a Cook's shop, under pretence of buying some meat; and while the Cook's back was turned, one of them snatched up a piece of beef, and gave it to his companion, who clapt it under his cloak. The Cook turning about, and missing his beef, began to charge them with it: upon which he that first took it swore bitterly he had none of it. He that had it, swore as heartily that he had not taken it. Why, look ye, gentlemen, says the Cook, I see your equivocation; and though I cannot tell which of you has taken my meat, I am sure between you there is a thief.

APPLICATION.

This fable shews how little reliance can be placed on either the word or the oath of those who, like the thieves in the cook's shop, have neither honour nor honesty. An honest man's word is as good as his oath; and so is a rogue's too: for he that will cheat and lie, will not scruple to forswear himself. The former needs no oath to bind him; and the latter, though he swear in the most solemn manner that can be invented, only deceives you the more certainly, as he who scruples not to steal, will never regard the heinous guilt of calling upon the Supreme Being to witness his atrocity. It is no less wicked to quibble and evade the truth, than it is to deny it altogether, for the falsehood consists in what we wish the hearer to believe, not in the literal import of what we say. Men who habituate themselves to this species of deceit, will soon be ready to go the length of any perjury. Early to impress the mind with the unspeakable worth of truth, is of the utmost importance. It is sacred, and no man can say in the face of the world, that it ought not to prevail. No discussions can injure its cause—it emanates from heaven—it is an attribute of omnipotence, and is therefore eternal.

THE MULE.

A Mule, which was pampered up and easily worked, became plump, sleek, and in high condition, and in the height of his wantonness, would scamper about from hill to dale in all the wildness of unbridled restraint. Why should not I, said he to himself, be as good a racer as any horse whatever? My father, whose pedigree was well known, was one of the best of them; do not I resemble him in every respect? While he was indulging his vanity in reveries of this kind, his master having occasion to mount him upon urgent business, put him upon his speed, and, ere long, was obliged to use both whip and spur to force him to push forward. Thus jaded and tired, he muttered to himself, Alas! I find now, I was mistaken in my pedigree, for my sire was not a Horse, but an Ass.

APPLICATION.

THE man who has been brought up in ease and affluence, and pampered and anticipated in all his wants, little imagines what a figure he would make in the world, were his supplies cut off, and he were put to the trial to rub through its thorny mazes, and provide for himself. The children of the poor industrious honest man, when brought up like their parents, are put to a kind of school, such as the opulent it is feared can seldom form any conception of; and if the former, by their industry and abilities, rise above poverty, their enjoyments in life commonly surpass those who have been, without effort, upheld in every real as well as imaginary want. The sensible poor man does not trouble his head about his pedigree, but he knows that his descent must of course be as ancient as that of any man on earth; and that if he is respected in the world, it must arise solely from his own good conduct and merit. The man who has nothing to boast but the merely tracing back his ancestry, is building upon a hollow foundation. If indeed his ancestry have arisen to their high station by patriotic and virtuous means, and have deservedly maintained a high character for probity, worth, and honour, let him follow their example: if otherwise, all he can do or say will only prove him to be a mongrel, or an ass.

" The pride of family is all a cheat,
" 'Tis personal merit only makes us great."

THE COCK AND THE JEWEL.

A gallant young Cock, in company with his mistresses, raking upon a dung-hill for something to entertain them with, happened to scratch up a Jewel. He knew what it was well enough, for it sparkled with an exceeding bright lustre; but not knowing what to do with it, he shrugged up his wings, shook his head, and putting on a grimace, expressed himself to this purpose: Indeed, you are a very fine thing; but I know not any business you have here. I make no scruple of declaring, that my taste lies quite another way; and I had rather have one grain of dear, delicious barley, than all the Jewels under the sun.

APPLICATION.

MORALISTS have interpreted this Fable in various

ways, some of them ascribing the want of setting a
proper value upon the Jewel, to ignorance, and say:—

" To fools, the treasures dug from wisdom's mine
" Are Jewels thrown to Cocks, and Pearls to Swine."

But the most obvious meaning of the Fable is surely
to shew, that men who weigh well their own real
wants, and shape their pursuits to their abilities, will
always prefer those things which are necessary, to such
as are merely ornamental or superfluous, and will not
easily suffer themselves to be led astray by the gaudy
allurements of glitter and show, which have no other
value than what vanity, pride, or luxury may have set
upon them; but governing their minds by their own
reason, judge of every thing by its intrinsic worth.

MERCURY AND THE WOODMAN.

A Man was felling a tree on the steep bank of a river, and by chance let slip his hatchet, which dropt into the water, and sunk to the bottom. Being in distress for want of his tool, he sat down and bemoaned himself on the occasion. Upon this, Mercury appeared to him, and being informed of the cause of his complaint, dived to the bottom of the river, and coming up again, shewed the Man a golden hatchet, demanding if that were his? he denied that it was: upon which Mercury dived a second time, and brought up a silver one; the Man refused it, alleging likewise that it was not his: he dived a third time, and fetched up the individual hatchet the Man had lost; upon sight of which the poor fellow was overjoyed, and took it with all humility and thankfulness. Mercury was so pleased with his honesty, that he gave him the other

H

into the bargain, as a reward for his just dealing. Away goes the Man to his companions, and giving them an account of what had happened, one of them went presently to the river's side, and let his hatchet fall designedly into the stream. Then sitting down upon the bank, he fell to weeping and lamenting as if he had been really and sorely afflicted. Mercury appeared as before, and diving, brought him up a golden hatchet, asking if that were the hatchet he had lost? Transported at the precious metal, he answered yes, and went to snatch it greedily; but the God, detesting his abominable impudence, not only refused him that, but would not so much as let him have his own again.

APPLICATION.

Honesty is the best policy; and one of our best poets has further stamped a value upon the good old maxim, by his assertion that " an honest man is the noblest work of God." The paths of truth and integrity are so plain, direct, and easy, that the man who pursues them, stands in no need of subtle contrivances to deceive the world. He listens to the honest monitor within, and makes good his professions with his practice: neither gold nor silver hatchets can make him deviate from it; and whatever situation he may be placed in, he is sure to meet the esteem of all men within the circle in which he moves, and has besides the constant pleasure of feeling self-approbation within his own breast.

THE FOX AND THE VIZOR MASK.

A Fox being in a shop where Vizor Masks were sold, laid his foot upon one of them, and considering it awhile attentively, at last broke out into this exclamation: Bless me! says he, what a handsome goodly figure this makes! what a pity it is that it should want brains!

APPLICATION.

The accomplished beau in air and mein how blest,
His hat well fashioned, and his hair well drest,
Is yet undrest within: to give him brains
Exceeds his hatter's or his barber's pains.

THIS Fable is levelled at that numerous part of man-kind, who, out of their own ample fortunes take care to accomplish themselves in every thing but common sense, and seem not even to bestow a thought upon the important consequences of cultivating their understandings. The smooth address and plausible behaviour of the varnished fop may indeed pass current with the ignorant and superficial, but however much he may value himself upon his birth or figure, he never fails exciting the contempt or the pity of men of sagacity and penetration, and the ridicule of those who are disposed to amuse themselves at the folly and vanity of such as put on the mask of wisdom to cover their want of brains.

THE THIEF AND THE DOG.

A Thief coming to rob a certain house in the night, was thwarted in his attempts by a fierce vigilant Dog, who kept barking at him continually. Upon which the Thief, thinking to stop his mouth, threw him a piece of bread; but the Dog refused it with indignation, telling him that before he only suspected him to be a bad man, but now upon his offering to bribe him, his suspicions were fully confirmed; and that as he was entrusted with the guardianship of his master's house, he would never cease barking while such a rogue was lurking about it.

APPLICATION.

NOTHING can alter the honest purpose of him whose mind is embued with good principles. He will despise an insidious bribe, and the greater the offer which is designed to buy his silence, the louder and more indignantly will he open out against the miscreant who would thus practise upon him. He knows that the favours held out to him are not marks of the love and regard of him who would confer them, but are meant as the price at which he is to sell his honour and his virtue.   With a mind unpolluted, his noble resolution never fails to produce the happiest consequences, by preserving his friends and himself from the mischievous projects laid against them.   So true it is, that virtue is its own reward; while corruption and venality are sure in the end to bring the greatest miseries on those, and their adherents, who are so base, or perhaps inconsiderate, as to subject themselves to future evils of the most fatal nature, for the sake of a little present profit.

THE MAN AND HIS GOOSE.

A certain Man had a Goose, which laid him a golden egg every day. But not contented with this, which rather increased than abated his avarice, he was resolved to kill the Goose, and cut up her belly, that by so doing he might come at the inexhaustible treasure which he fancied she had within her. He did so, and to his great sorrow and disappointment, found nothing.

APPLICATION.

No passion can be a greater torment to those who are led by it, or more frequently mistakes its aim, than insatiable covetousness. It makes men blind to their present happiness, and conjures up ideal prospects of increasing felicity, which often tempt its deluded votaries to their ruin. Men who give themselves up to

this propensity, know not how to be contented with
the constant and continued sufficiency with which
Providence may have blessed them: their minds are
haunted with the prospect of becoming rich, and their
impatient craving tempers are perpetually prompting
them to try to obtain their object all at once.   They
lose all present enjoyment in remotely contemplating
the future; and while they are shewing by their conduct how insensible they are to the bounty of Providence, they are at the same time laying the foundation
of their own unhappiness.

THE WANTON CALF.

A Calf, which had been some time fattening in a rich pasture, full of wantonness and arrogance, could not forbear insulting an old Ox every time he saw him at the plough. What a sorry drudge art thou, says he, to bear that heavy yoke, and draw all day a plough at thy tail! See, what a fat, sleek, and comely appearance I make, and what a life of ease I lead: I go where I please, and frisk about in the sunshine, or lie down under the cool shade, just as my own fancy prompts me. The Ox, not moved by this insolence, made no reply, but pursued his daily round of alternate labour and rest, until he saw the Calf taken and delivered to a priest, who immediately led him to the altar, and prepared to sacrifice him. When the fatal knife was just at his throat, the Ox drew near, and whispered him to this purpose: see what your wanton

I

and lazy life has brought you to, a premature and painful death.

APPLICATION.

WE may learn by this Fable the general consequence of an idle life, and how well rewarded laborious diligent men are in the end, when they quietly
enjoy the fruits of their industry. They who by little
tricks and chicanery, or by open violence and robbery,
are enabled to live in a high expensive way, often despise the poor honest man, who is contented with the
humble produce of his daily labour. But how often
is the poor man comforted, by seeing these wanton
villains led in disgrace and misery to the altar of justice, while he has many a cheerful summer's morning
to enjoy abroad, and many a long winter's evening to
indulge in at home, by a quiet hearth, and under an
unenvied roof: blessings, which often attend a sober
industrious man, though the idle and the profligate
are utter strangers to them. Luxury and intemperance, besides their inevitable tendency to shorten a
man's days, are very apt to engage their besotted
votaries in a debauched life, not only prejudicial to
their health, but which engenders in them a contempt for those whose good sense and true taste of
happiness inspire them with an aversion to idleness
and effeminacy, and put them upon hardening their
constitution by innocent exercise and laudable employment. How many do gluttony and sloth tumble
into an untimely grave ! while the temperate and the
active drink sober draughts of life, and spin out the
thread of their existence to the most desirable length.

THE BOASTING TRAVELLER.

ONE who had been abroad, was giving an account of his travels, and among other places, said he had been at Rhodes, where he had distinguished himself so much in leaping, an exercise which that city was famous for, that not a Rhodian could come near him. When those who were present did not seem to credit this relation so readily as he intended they should, he took some pains to convince them of it by oaths and protestations: upon which, one of the company told him he need not give himself so much trouble about it, since he would put him in a way to demonstrate the fact; which was, to suppose the place they were in to be Rhodes, and to perform his extraordinary leap over again. The boaster, not liking this proposal, sat down quietly, and had no more to say for himself.

APPLICATION.

WE had better be contented to keep our exploits to ourselves, than to appear ridiculous by attempting to force a belief of that which is improbable; and travelled gentlemen should have a care how they import falsehoods and inventions of their own from foreign parts, and attempt to vend them at home for staple truths. It cannot be too strongly impressed upon the mind, that a lie is upon all occasions degrading to the person who utters it, and should be most scrupulously avoided, not only on account of its baseness, but because it is impossible to foresee in how many troubles it may involve him who passes it off. It will not always receive credit, and is ever liable to detection. When it is calculated for wicked purposes, it will deservedly incur punishment; and when it is of a harmless or insignificant nature, it will even then often expose its author to contempt and ridicule; and vanity never mistakes its end more grossly, than when it attempts to aggrandize itself at the expence of truth.

THE SHEPHERD'S BOY AND THE WOLF.

A Shepherd's Boy, while attending his flock, used frequently to divert himself by crying out, " the Wolf! the Wolf!" The Husbandmen in the adjoining grounds, thus alarmed, left their work and ran to his assistance, but finding that he was only sporting with their feelings, and bantering them, they resolved at last to take no notice of his alarms. It was not long, however, before the Wolf really came, and the Boy bawled out " the Wolf! the Wolf!" as he had done before; but the men having been so often deceived, paid no attention to his cries, and the sheep were devoured without mercy.

APPLICATION.

THE man who would go through the world with

reputation and success, must preserve a religious adherence to truth: for no talents or industry can give him weight with others, or induce the sensible part of mankind to place any confidence in him, if he be known to deviate without scruple from veracity. Men of this stamp soon become notorious; and besides the ignominy which attaches to their characters, they have to undergo the mortification of not being believed even when they do speak the truth. Whatever misfortune may befal them, and however sincere they may be in making known their distress, yet, like the boy in the Fable, their complaints and most earnest asseverations cannot procure them credit, and are received at best with doubt and suspicion. The same consequences follow falsehood and deception, whether practised by individuals or public governors, and they will both find in the end that they have been guided by cunning, and not by wisdom: for although the ignorant part of mankind may, to serve the temporary purposes of a bad government, be acted upon by false alarms of imaginary dangers, yet even these in time will see through the stale tricks and artifices of those whose designs are to gull and impose upon them.

This Stone, like many
100000 of men in the world
has held up its bare
useless head for many
Centuries past

THE CROW AND THE PITCHER.

A Crow, ready to die with thirst, flew with joy to a Pitcher which he beheld at some distance. When he came, he found water in it, indeed, but so near the bottom, that with all his stooping and straining, he was not able to reach it. He then endeavoured to overturn the Pitcher, that at least he might be able to get a little of it; but his strength was not sufficient for the accomplishment of this purpose. At last seeing some pebbles lie near the place, he cast them one by one into the Pitcher, and thus, by degrees, raised the water up to the very brim, and satisfied his thirst.

APPLICATION.

WHAT we cannot accomplish by strength, we may by ingenuity and industry. A man of sagacity and penetration, upon meeting with a few difficulties, does not drop his pursuits, but if he cannot succeed in one way, sets his mind to work upon another, and does not hesitate about stepping out of the old beaten track which had been thoughtlessly pursued in a roundabout way by thousands before him. The present state of the world, enlightened by arts and sciences, is a proof that difficulties seemingly unsurmountable, and undertakings once imagined to be impossible, have been accomplished; and this ought to be kept in mind as a spur to continued exertion: for we are not acquainted with the strength of our own minds till we exercise them, nor to what length our abilities will carry us, till we put them to the trial.

   " What is discovered only serves to shew,
   That nothing's known to what is yet to know."

The man who enriches the present fund of knowledge with some new and useful improvement, does an honour to himself, and ought invariably to be rewarded by the public: for, like a happy adventurer by sea, he discovers as it were an unknown land, and imports an additional treasure to his own country.

THE PARTRIDGE AND THE COCKS.

A Man having caught a Partridge, plucked the feathers out of one of its wings, and turned it into a little yard where he kept Game Cocks. The Cocks led the poor bird a sad life, continually pecking at and driving it away from the meat. This treatment was taken the more unkindly, because offered to a stranger; and the Partridge could not help concluding that they were the most uncivil inhospitable people he had ever met with. But observing how very frequently they quarrelled and fought with each other, he comforted himself with reflecting, that it was no wonder they were so cruel to him, since they shewed the same disposition to each other.

K

APPLICATION.

No peace is to be expected among those who are
naturally fierce, quarrelsome, and inhospitable; and
people of a different disposition should avoid, as much
as possible, having any thing to do with them. But
when we cannot help coming into contact with such
characters, there is no remedy but patience; and this
virtue a wise man will call to his aid under every misfortune. When our sufferings are inflicted by the
wickedness of others, it is some consolation to reflect,
that people of this character are continually waging
war among themselves, and punishing each other; and
that the consequences of their own wickedness follow
them like their shadow, besides rendering them the
objects of general aversion. No virtue was more universally practised, or more strongly recommended, by
the ancients, than a mild conduct to our companions,
and an hospitable entertainment of strangers; and
when this is not the general character of any people,
it shews, in greater or less degrees, the wretched state
of society in which they live.

THE FOX AND THE CROW.

A Crow having taken a piece of meat out of a cottage window, flew up into a tree with it; which a Fox observing, came underneath, and began to compliment the Crow upon her beauty. I protest, says he, your feathers are of a more delicate white than I ever saw in my life! Ah! what a fine shape and graceful turn of body is there! and I make no question but you have a tolerable voice: if it be but as fine as your complexion, I do not know a bird that can stand in competition with you. The Crow, tickled with this very civil language, wriggled about, and hardly knew where she was; and having a mind to convince the Fox in the matter of her voice, attempted to sing, and in the same instant let the meat drop out of her mouth. This being what the Fox wanted, he

chopped it up in a moment, and trotted away, laughing at the easy credulity of the Crow.

APPLICATION.

" It is a maxim in the schools,
That flattery is the food of fools."

THEY that love flattery will have cause to repent
of their foible in the long run; and yet how few there
are among the whole race of mankind, who are proof
against its attacks. The gross way in which it is managed by some silly practitioners, is enough to alarm
the dullest apprehension; but let the ambuscade be
disposed with judgment, and it will scarcely fail of
seizing the most guarded heart. How many are tickled
to the last degree with the pleasure of flattery, even
while they are applauded for their honest detestation
of it. There is no way to baffle the force of this en-
gine, but by every one's examining impartially for
himself, the true estimate of his own qualities. If he
deal sincerely in the matter, nobody can tell so well
as himself, what degree of esteem ought to attend any
of his actions; and therefore he should be entirely
easy as to the opinion others have of them. If they
attribute more to him than is his due, they are either
designing, or mistaken; if they allow him less, they
are envious, or possibly still mistaken; and in either
case are to be despised or disregarded: for he that
flatters without designing to make advantage of it, is a
fool; and whoever encourages that flattery which he
has sense enough to see through, is a vain coxcomb.

THE SENSIBLE ASS.

AN old Man who was feeding his Ass in a fine
green meadow, being alarmed by the sudden approach
of an enemy, began urging the Ass to put himself forward, and fly with all the speed he was able. The
Ass asked him whether he thought the enemy would
clap two pair of panniers upon his back? The Man
said, No, there was no fear of that. Why then, says
the Ass, I will not stir an inch, for what is it to me
who my master is, since I shall but carry my panniers
as usual.

APPLICATION.

THIS Fable shews us how much in the wrong the
poorer sort of people most commonly are, when they

are under any concern about the revolutions of a government. All the alteration which they can feel, is
perhaps in the name of their sovereign, or some such
important trifle; but they cannot well be poorer, or
made to work harder, than they did before. And yet
how are they sometimes imposed upon and drawn in
by the artifices of a few mistaken or designing men,
to foment factions, and raise rebellions, in cases where
they can get nothing by success; but if they miscarry,
are in danger of suffering an ignominious and untimely end.

THE SWALLOW AND OTHER BIRDS.

A Swallow, observing a Farmer sowing his field with flax, called the Birds together, and informed them what he was about. She told them that flax was the material of which the thread was made that composed the fowler's nets, so fatal to the feathered race, and strongly advised them to assist her in picking up the seed, and destroying it. The Birds heard her with indifference, and gave themselves no trouble about the matter. In a little time the flax sprung up, and appeared above the ground. She then put them in mind once more of their impending danger, and wished them to pluck it up in the bud, before it grew any farther. But they still slighted her warnings, and the flax grew up into stalk. She again urged them to attack it, for it was not yet too late; but they only ridiculed her for a silly pretending prophet. The

Swallow, finding all her remonstrances availed nothing, was resolved to leave the society of such careless
unthinking creatures, before it was too late: so quit-
ting the woods, she repaired to the houses; and, for-·
saking the conversation of the Birds, has ever since
taken up her abode among the dwellings of men.

APPLICATION.

Wise men read effects in their causes, and profit
by them; but their advice is thrown away when given
to the arrogant and self-conceited, who are too proud
to listen to it. It is equally lost upon fools, who stupidly or obstinately shut their eyes against impending
danger, till it is too late to prevent it. In both cases,
those who have no foresight of their own, and those
who despise the wholesome admonitions of their friends,
deserve to suffer from the misfortunes which their
own obstinacy, folly, or negligence, brings upon their
heads. A great portion of mankind, from an over-
weening conceit of their own abilities, are unwilling
to be advised by any one, and through this stubborn
disposition, deprive themselves of the aids of friendship, and the benefits which the good-will of their
more sensible neighbours would have conferred on
them with pleasure.

THE THIEVES AND THE COCK.

Two Thieves broke into a house with a design to rob it; but when they had pried into every corner, found nothing worth taking away but a Cock, which they seized upon and carried off. When they were about to kill him, he begged very hard that they would spare his life, putting them in mind how useful he was to mankind, by crowing and calling them up betimes to their work. You villain, replied they, it is for that very reason we will wring your head off; for you alarm and keep the people waking, so that we cannot rob in quiet for you.

APPLICATION.

THE same thing which recommends us to the esteem of good people, will make those that are bad have nothing but hatred and ill-will towards us; for every man

L

who has engaged himself in a vicious or wicked course
of life, fiend-like, makes himself, as it were, the natural adversary of virtue. It is in vain for innocent
men, under oppression, to complain to those who are
the occasion of it: all they can urge will but make
against them; and even their very innocence, though
they should say nothing, would render them sufficiently suspected. The moral, therefore, that this Fable
brings along with it, is to inform us that there is no
trusting, nor any hopes of living well, with wicked unjust men; for their disposition is such, that they will
do mischief to others as soon as they have the opportunity. When vice flourishes, and is in power, were
it possible for a good man to live quietly in its neighbourhood, and preserve his integrity, it might be sometimes perhaps convenient for him to do so, rather than
quarrel with and provoke it against him. But as it is
certain that rogues are irreconcileable enemies to men
of worth, if the latter would be secure, they must take
methods to free themselves from the power and society
of the former.

THE WOLVES AND THE SICK ASS.

An Ass being sick, the report was spread abroad in the country, and some did not scruple to say, that she would die before another night went over her head. Upon this, several Wolves went to the stable where she lay, under pretence of making her a visit; but rapping at the door, and asking how she did, the young Ass came out, and told them that his mother was much better than they desired.

APPLICATION.

If the kind enquiries after the sick were all to be interpreted with as much frankness as those in the Fable, the porters of the great might commonly answer with the strictest propriety, that their masters were much better than was wished or desired. The

L 2

charitable visits which are made to many sick people, proceed from much the same motive with that which induced the hungry Wolves to make their enquiries after the sick Ass, namely, that they may come in for some share of their remains, and feast themselves upon the reversion of their goods and chattels. The sick man's heir longs for his estate; one friend waits in anxious expectation of a legacy, and another wants his place; it, however, does not unfrequently happen, that the mask of these selfish visitants, and their counterfeit sorrow, are seen through, and their impertinent officiousness treated with the contempt it so justly deserves.

'Tis the world! floating about, like an illumined mote, in the immensity of endless space — and is inhabited by nations of proud Pismires. —

THE DOG IN THE MANGER.

A Dog was lying upon a stall full of hay. An Ox, being hungry, came near, and offered to eat of the hay; but the ill-natured Cur getting up and snarling at him, would not suffer him to touch it. Upon which the Ox, in the bitterness of his heart, said, A curse light on thee for a malicious wretch, who will neither eat hay thyself, nor suffer others to do it.

APPLICATION.

THERE are men in the world of so snarling, malevolent, and ill-natured a disposition, that they will even punish themselves, rather than put forth a finger to serve any one. It gives them a malignant kind of pleasure to have it in their power to cause trouble and vexation to others, whenever they have an opportunity of doing so; and could they have their will, they would shut out the light and warmth of the sun, and suffer the fruits of the earth to rot upon it, provided they could see those about them unhappy; and in thus taking delight in other people's miseries, it of course follows that they are their own tormentors. These characters, in common life, are diabolical and detestable; but the evils they inflict, are only like a drop to the ocean, when compared to those which men of the same stamp shed abroad in the world, when, in an evil hour, they happen to be exalted to govern the affairs of a nation. Then, indeed, their baleful influence is felt in every direction: they may be termed fiends in human shape; for, as far as they are able, they thwart the benevolent intentions of Omnipotence, and the very breath of their nostrils seems to blast the happiness of mankind.

JUPITER AND THE ASS.

An Ass which had been some time in the service of a Gardener, and carried his vegetables to market, became tired of his place, and petitioned Jupiter that he would permit him to enter upon the service of a neighbouring Potter. Jupiter granted his request. He here, however, soon found that the latter loaded him with heavier burthens, and kept him on poorer fare than he had been used to before. He again prayed to Jupiter to grant that he might be allowed to better his condition by engaging himself to a Tanner. Jupiter again heard his prayer; but here he soon found he had changed for the worse: for, besides being hard worked, he was also often cruelly treated; and seeing what was going on in this place, he could not forbear upbraiding himself with his folly and inconstancy. Oh, tofo that I was! said he to himself, for leaving my former mild master, to become the servant of one, who, after working me to death, will not spare my very hide after I am dead.

APPLICATION.

THE man that carries about with him the plague of a restless mind, can never be pleased; he is ever shifting and changing, and is in truth not so weary of his condition as of himself. Seldom or never contented with his lot, he is ever hunting after happiness where it is not to be found, without ever looking for it where it is. He indulges in the strange propensity of his nature, which leads him to suppose that his own lot is the most miserable, and therefore concludes that any change he can make must be for the better. He loses sight of the virtues of patience, constancy, and resignation, and seems not to know that every station in life has its real or imaginary inconveniences; and that it is better to bear with those which we are accustomed to endure, and of which we know the utmost extent, than by aiming at the seeming advantages of another way of life, to subject ourselves to all its hidden miseries.

ÆSOP AND THE IMPERTINENT FELLOW.

Æsop having occasion to go out to seek a light to kindle his fire, went from house to house for some time before he could succeed; but having at last got what he wanted, he posted back in haste with his lighted candle in his hand. An impudent Fellow, leaving his companions, caught hold of Æsop by the sleeve, and would fain have shewn off his wit, and been arch upon him. Hey day! oh, rare Æsop! says he, what occasion for a candle, old boy! what, are you going to light the sun to bed? Let me alone, says Æsop, for with it I am looking for an honest man.

APPLICATION.

It is plain that our old philosopher in the Fable did not take the impertinent fellow for an honest man,

M

and he gave him to understand that it required a good
light to find out one who fully came up to that character; and he might have added, that the world very
much abounded with ignorant and impudent ones,
who, with their empty nonsense, which they call wit,
often unseasonably interrupt men of thought and business: for to those whose minds are wholly intent upon
matters of importance, nothing is so offensive as the
intrusion of a fool. Men of eminent parts and great
natural abilities, make their appearance in the world
only now and then. These qualifications are the gift
of Providence, and seem to be intended to throw fresh
lights on the understandings of mankind; but in all the
gradations from these downwards, it is in the power
of every one to improve their manners, and integrity
is within the reach of those of the meanest capacity, if
they will endeavour to amend their lives, and take it
for their guide.

THE FORESTER AND THE LION.

THE Forester meeting with the Lion one day, they discoursed together for a while without much differing in opinion. At last, a dispute happening to arise about the point of superiority between a Man and a Lion, the former wanting a better argument, shewed the latter a marble monument, on which was placed the statue of a Man striding over a vanquished Lion. If this, says the Lion, is all you have to say for it, let us be the sculptors, and we will make the Lion striding over the Man.

APPLICATION.

SUCH is the partiality of mankind in favour of themselves and their own actions, that it is extremely

M 2

difficult, nay almost impossible to come at any certainty, by reading the accounts that are written on
one side only. The simple truth is still perverted, as
prejudice, vanity, or interest warps the mind, and it
is not discovered in all its brilliancy, till the mists
which obscure it are swept away by the most rigid investigation. In what an odious light would our party
men place each other, if the transactions of the times
were handed down to posterity by a warm zealot on
either side; and were such records to survive a few
centuries, with what perplexities and difficulties would
they embarrass the historian, as by turns he consulted
them for the character of his great forefathers. The
same difficulties would occur in writing the history of
nations, both ancient and modern. Some of those
who flourish at this day, and consider themselves as
having reached perfection in civilization and polished
manners, will perhaps, not unjustly, be branded in
after-times with cruelty, injustice, and oppression, in
having confounded all simplicity of manners, and disturbed the peace of whole nations, by carrying the
horrors of war, of murder, and desolation, into regions formerly blessed with uninterrupted tranquillity.

THE WOLF, THE FOX, AND THE APE.

THE Wolf indicted the Fox for felony before the Ape, who upon that occasion was appointed special judge of the cause. The Fox gave in his answer to the Wolf's accusation, and denied the fact. After hearing both sides, the Ape, penetrating the character of the parties, gave judgment to this purpose: I am of opinion, that you, says he to the Wolf, never lost the goods you sue for; and as for you, turning to the Fox, I make no question but you at least have stolen what is laid to your charge. And thus the court was dismissed with this public censure upon each party.

APPLICATION.

WELL may both judge and jury, in the outset of trial, be puzzled to decide between and do justice to men whose quarrels are made up of baseness and villainy, and carried on with mutual treachery, fraud, and violence, and whose witnesses are perhaps of the same character with themselves. Each party may justly enough accuse the other, though neither of them are worthy of belief, and deserve even no credit for the imputations with which they asperse each other's characters. But such men need not hope long to deceive the world: a penetrating judge and an honest jury will, upon sifting the matter, clearly see what kind of men they have been occupying their attention with, and shew a proper disgust at the wicked impudence of both plaintiff and defendant.

THE BALD KNIGHT.

A certain Knight growing old, his hair fell off, and he became bald; to hide which imperfection he wore a periwig. But as he was riding out with some others a hunting, a sudden gust of wind blew off the periwig, and exposed his bald pate. The company could not forbear laughing at the accident; and he himself laughed as loud as any body, saying, how was it to be expected that I could keep strange hair upon my head, when my own would not stay there?

APPLICATION.

THERE is no disposition, or turn of mind, which on many occasions contributes more to keep us easy, than that which enables us to rally any of our failings, or joke upon our own infirmities: this blunts the edge, and baffles and turns aside the malignant sneers of little wits, and the ill nature and ridicule of others. If we should at any time happen to incur the laughter of those about us, we cannot stifle it sooner or better than by receiving it all with a cheerful look, and by an ingenuous and pleasant remark, parry the jest which another is ready to throw out at our expence. To appear fretted or nettled, only serves to gratify the wishes of those who take a secret pleasure in seeing such an effect produced; and, besides, a testy or captious temper is a source of perpetual disquietude, both to ourselves and our acquaintances, and like a little leaven, sours the whole mass of our good qualities. If we had no other imperfections, this of itself would be sufficient to cause our company to be shunned.

THE LION AND THE FOUR BULLS.

Four Bulls, who had entered into a very strict friendship, kept always near one another, and fed together. The Lion often saw them, and as often had a mind to make one of them his prey; but though he could easily have subdued any of them singly, yet he was afraid to attack the whole alliance, knowing they would have been too powerful for him, and therefore was obliged to keep himself at a distance. At last, perceiving that no attempt was to be made upon them as long as their combination lasted, he artfully contrived, by the whispers and hints of his emissaries, to foment jealousies, and raise divisions among them. This stratagem succeeded so well, that the Bulls grew cold and reserved to one another, which soon after ripened into a downright hatred and aversion, and at last ended in a total separation. The Lion had now

N

attained his ends; and though it had been impossible
for him to hurt them while they were united, he found
no difficulty, now they were parted, to seize and devour
every Bull of them, one after another.

APPLICATION.

Since friendships and alliances are of the greatest
importance to our well-being and happiness, we cannot be too often cautioned against suffering them to
be broken by tale bearers and whisperers, or by any
dark plots and contrivances of our enemies: for when
by such wicked means as these, or by our own imprudence, we lose a friend, we shake the very basis
of our interest, and remove the pillar that contributed
to support it.   Whatever in cases of this kind is applicable to individuals, is equally so to kingdoms and
states; and it is as undisputed a maxim as ever was
urged upon the attention of mankind, by the best man
that ever lived, that a " kingdom divided against itself
cannot stand :" the people are invincible when united.

Faction and feuds will overturn the state
Which union renders flourishing and great.

THE OLD MAN AND HIS SONS.

An old Man had several Sons, who were constantly quarrelling with each other, notwithstanding he used every means in his power to persuade them to cease their contentions, and to live in amity together. At last he had recourse to the following expedient:— He ordered his Sons to be called before him, and a bundle of sticks to be brought, and then commanded them to try if, with all their strength, any of them could break it. They all tried, but without effect: for the sticks being closely and compactly bound together, it was impossible for the force of man to break them. After this, the Father ordered the bundle to be untied, and gave a single stick to each of his Sons, at the same time bidding them try to break it. This they did with ease, and soon snapped every stick asunder. The Father then addressed them to this effect:

O, my Sons, behold the power of unity! for if you, in like manner, would but keep yourselves strictly conjoined in the bands of friendship, it would not be in the power of any mortal to hurt you; but when you are divided by quarrels and animosities, you fall a prey to the weakest enemies.

APPLICATION.

A kingdom divided against itself is brought to desolation; and the same holds good in all societies and corporations of men, from the constitution of the nation, down to every little parochial vestry. Every private family should consider itself a little state, in which the several members ought to be united by one common interest. Quarrels with each other are as fatal to their welfare, as factions are dangerous to the peace of the commonwealth. But indeed the necessity of union and friendship extends itself to all kinds of relations in life, and they conduce mightily to the advantage of those who cherish and cultivate them. No enemy will dare to attack a body of men firmly attached to each other, and will fear to offend one of the number, lest he should incur the resentment of the rest; but if they split into parties, and are disunited by quarrels, every petty opponent will venture to attack them, and the whole fraternity will be liable to wrongs and violence.

THE LION, THE TIGER, AND THE WOLF.

A Lion and a Tiger, at the same instant seized on a young Fawn, which they immediately killed. This they had no sooner performed, than they fell to fighting, in order to decide whose property it should be. The battle was so obstinate, that they were both compelled, by weariness and loss of blood, to desist and lie down breathless and quite disabled. A Wolf passing that way, perceiving how the case stood, very impudently stepped up and seized the booty, which they had all this while been contending for, and carried it off. The two combatants, who beheld this without being able to prevent it, could only make this reflection: How foolish, said they, has been our conduct! Instead of being contented, as we ought, with our respective shares, our senseless rage has rendered us

unable to prevent this rascally Wolf from robbing us
of the whole.

APPLICATION.

When people go to law about an uncertain title,
and have spent the value of their whole estate in the
contest, nothing is more common than to find that
some unprincipled attorney has secured the object in
dispute to himself. The very name of law seems to
imply equity and justice, and that is the bait which
has drawn in many to their ruin. If we would lay
aside passion, prejudice, and folly, and think calmly of
the matter, we should find that going to law is not
the best way of deciding differences about property; it
being, generally speaking, much safer to trust to the
arbitration of two or three honest sensible neighbours,
than at a vast expence of money, time, and trouble,
to run through the tedious frivolous forms, with which,
by the artifices of greedy lawyers, a court of judica-
ture is contrived to be attended. Or if a case should
happen to be so intricate that a man of common sense
cannot distinguish who has the best title, how easy
would it be to have the opinion of the best counsel in
the land, and agree to abide by his decision. If it
should appear dubious, even after that, how much
better would it be to divide the thing in dispute, rather
than go to law, and hazard the losing, not only of the
whole, but costs and damages into the bargain !

THE FOX WITHOUT A TAIL.

A Fox being caught in a trap, escaped after much difficulty with the loss of his tail. He was, however, a good deal ashamed of appearing in public without this ornament, and at last, to avoid being singular and ridiculous in the eyes of his own species, he formed the project of calling together an assembly of Foxes, and of persuading them that the docking of their tails was a fashion that would be very agreeable and becoming. Accordingly he made a long harangue to them for that purpose, and endeavoured chiefly to shew the awkwardness and inconvenience of a Fox's tail, adding that they were quite useless, and that they would be a very great deal better without them. He asserted, that what he had only conjectured and imagined before, he now found by experience to be true, for he never enjoyed himself so much, and found himself so easy as he had done since he cut off his tail. He then looked round with a brisk air, to see what proselytes he had gained; when a sly old Fox in company answered him, with a leer: I believe you may have found a convenience in parting with your tail, and perhaps when we are in the same circumstances, we may do so too.

APPLICATION.

MANY of the fashions which obtain in the world, originate in the whim or caprice of some vain conceited creature, who takes a pride in leading the giddy multitude in a career of folly. Others again take their rise from an artful design to cover some vice, or hide some deformity in the person of the inventor. Projectors and planners of a higher stamp are also not uncommon in the world. These men appear to toil only for the public good, and the sacred name of patriotism is their shield. It, however, often happens that when their deep schemes are opened out, they are found to proceed from nothing better than self-interested motives, and a sincere desire to serve themselves.

THE MISER AND HIS TREASURE.

A certain Miser, having got together a large sum of money, sought out a sequestered spot, where he dug a hole and hid it. His greatest pleasure was to go and look upon his treasure; which one of his servants observing, and guessing there was something more than ordinary in the place, came at night, found the hoard, and carried it off. The next day, the Miser returning as usual to the scene of his delight, and perceiving the money gone, tore his hair for grief, and uttered the most dolcful accents of despair. A neighbour, who knew his temper, overhearing him, said, Cheer up, man! thou hast lost nothing: there is still a hole to peep at: and if thou canst but fancy the money there, it will do just as well.

APPLICATION.

OF all the appetites to which human nature is subject, none is so lasting, so strong, and so unaccountable, as avarice. Other desires generally cool at the approach of old age; but this flourishes under grey hairs, and triumphs amidst infirmities. All our other longings have something to be said in excuse for them; but it is above reason, and therefore truly incomprehensible, why a man should be passionately fond of money only for the sake of gazing upon it. His treasure is as useless to him as a heap of oyster shells; for though he knows how many substantial pleasures it might procure, yet he dares not touch it, and is as destitute, to all intents and purposes, as the man who is not worth a groat. This is the true state of a covetous person, to which one of that fraternity perhaps may reply, that when we have said all, since pleasure is the grand aim of life, if there arise a delight to some, from the bare possession of riches, though they do not use, or even intend to use them, we may be puzzled how to account for it, and think it strange, but ought not absolutely to condemn those who thus closely, but innocently, pursue what they esteem the greatest happiness. True! people would be in the wrong to paint covetousness in such odious colours, were it compatible with innocence. But here arises the mischief: a covetous man will stop at nothing to attain his ends; and when once avarice takes the field, honesty, charity, humanity, and every virtue which opposes it, are sure to be put to the rout.

THE SHIP DOG.

A young saucy Dog, having been found not to like any employment at home, was taken by a sea captain on board his ship, where, being well fed, he soon became both stout and fierce, and shewed himself off as such in every foreign port. He no sooner got ashore, than he held up his leg against every post and corner, and scraped the ground with his feet, quite regardless what dog he might bespatter; and if any of them happened to look sulkily at him, he thought nothing of seizing upon and rolling them in the kennel. If he happened to fall into company, he always began to give himself airs, to talk big, and to express his contempt for the dogs of the place. He would boast that he was from a better country, and belonged to a better family than any dog among them. In short, said he, " I come from Cheviot, the highest mountain in the world, and the very heart of all England, where my forefathers, thousands of years ago, assembled to hunt the Wild Bull, the Wolf, and the Boar." He was once going on at this rate, when he was interrupted by a sedate, experienced Bitch, who assured him that there were good dogs and bad dogs in every country, and that the only difference arose from their education; that many of the forefathers he boasted of, had long since worried each other, and the remainder of them had become so troublesome, that part had been transported across the sea to another place; and she knew, from good authority, that both his father and his mother were hanged.

APPLICATION.

WHEN foreigners speak slightingly of the country they happen to be in, and praise their own, it shews in them a want of good sense and good breeding. It is indeed natural to have an affection for one's native land, nor can we help preferring it to every other; but to express this in another country, to people whose opinion it must needs contradict, by the same rule that it is conformable to our own, cannot fail of giving them just offence. It matters not how highly some particular countries may stand in the estimation of the rest of the world: this has little to do with private individuals; the advantage of having been born in one of those favoured countries, is accidental, and no man ought to be esteemed merely on that account. In order to merit the respect of virtuous and wise men in every foreign land, it must appear to them that by our talents, our acquirements, and our patriotism, we do credit to the country which gave us birth.

THE GOAT AND THE LION.

THE Lion, seeing a Goat upon a steep craggy rock, where he could not come at him, asked him what delight he could take to skip from one precipice to another all day, and venture the breaking of his neck every moment? I wonder, says he, you will not come down and feed on the plain here, when there is such plenty of grass, and fine sweet herbs. Why, replies the Goat, I cannot but say your opinion is right; but you look so very hungry and designing, that, to tell you the truth, I do not care to venture my person where you are.

APPLICATION.

ADVICE, though good in itself, is to be suspected when it is given by a tricking, self-interested man.

Perhaps we should take upon ourselves not only a very great, but an unnecessary trouble, if we were to suspect every man who offers to advise us; but this however is necessary, that when we have reason to question any one in point of honour and justice, we not only consider well before we suffer ourselves to be persuaded by him, but even resolve to have nothing to do in any affair where such treacherous slippery sparks are concerned, if we can avoid it without much inconvenience.

THE TWO TRAVELLERS.

Two Men travelling upon the road, one of them saw an Axe lying upon the ground, where somebody had been hewing timber: so taking it up, says he, I have found an Axe. Do not say I, says the other, but we have found; for as we are companions, we ought to share the value between us: but the first would not consent. They had not gone far, before the owner of the Axe, hearing what was become of it, pursued them with a warrant; which, when the fellow that had it, perceived, Alas! says he to his companion, we are undone. Nay, says the other, do not say we, but I am undone: for, as you would not let me share the prize, neither will I share the danger with you.

APPLICATION.

We cannot reasonably expect those to bear a part in our ill-fortune, whom we never permitted to share in our prosperity; and whoever is so over-selfish and narrow-minded, as to exclude his friend from a portion of the benefits to which an intimate connection entitles him, may, perhaps, engross some petty advantages to himself, but he must lay his account on being left to do as well as he can for himself in times of difficulty and distress. The very life and soul of friendship subsist upon mutual benevolence, and in conferring and receiving obligations on either hand, with a free, open, and unreserved behaviour, without the least tincture of jealousy, suspicion, or distrust, guided by a strict observance of the rules of honour and generosity; and as no man includes within himself every thing necessary for his security, defence, preservation, and support, these rules are the requisites of friendship, to make it firm and lasting, and the foundation on which it must be built.

THE FOX AND THE ASS.

An Ass finding a Lion's skin, disguised himself in it, and ranged about the forest, putting all the beasts in bodily fear. After he had diverted himself thus for some time, he met a Fox, and being desirous to frighten him too, as well as the rest, he leapt at him with some fierceness, and endeavoured to imitate the roaring of a Lion. Your humble servant, says the Fox, if you had held your tongue, I might have taken you for a Lion, as others did, but now you bray, I know who you are.

APPLICATION.

A man is known by his words, as a tree is by the fruit; and if we would be apprized of the nature and qualities of any one, let him but discourse, and he

P

will speak them to us better than another can describe them. We may therefore perceive, from this Fable, how proper it is for those to hold their tongues, who would not discover the shallowness of their understandings. " Empty vessels make the greatest sound," and the deepest rivers are most silent; the greatest noise is ever found where there is the least depth of water. It is a true observation, that those who are the weakest in understanding, and most slow of apprehension, are generally the most precipitate in uttering their crude conceptions. Grave looks, an aspect of dignity, and a solemn deportment, may sometimes deceive even an accurate observer; but wise discourse cannot be successfully counterfeited or assumed, and the sententious blockhead is as easily recognised as the pert coxcomb. It matters not what disguise one of these may assume; he utters himself, and undeceives us: he brays, and tells the whole company what he is.

THE CAT AND THE FOX.

As the Cat and the Fox were once talking politics together, in the middle of a forest, Reynard said, let things turn out ever so bad, he did not care, for he had a thousand tricks for them yet, before they should hurt him; but pray, says he, Mrs Puss, suppose there should be an invasion, what course do you design to take? Nay, says the Cat, I have but one shift for it, and if that wont do, I am undone. I am sorry for you, replies Reynard, with all my heart, and would gladly furnish you with one or two of mine; but indeed neighbour, as times go, it is not good to trust, we must even be every one for himself, as the saying is, and so your humble servant. These words were scarcely out of his mouth, when they were alarmed with a pack of hounds, that came upon them in full cry. The Cat, by the help of her single shift, ran up a tree and sat securely among the branches, whence she beheld Reynard, who had not been able to get out of sight, overtaken with his thousand tricks, and torn into as many pieces by the Dogs, which had surrounded him.

APPLICATION.

ONE good discreet expedient made use of upon an emergency, will do a man more real service, and make others think better of him, than to have passed all his life for a shrewd crafty fellow, full of his stratagems and expedients, and valuing himself upon his having a deeper knowledge of the world than his neighbours. Plain good sense, and a downright honest meaning, are a better guide through life, and more trusty security against danger, than the low shifts of cunning, and the refinements of artifice. Cunning is of a deep entangling nature, and is a sign of a small genius; though when it happens to be successful, it often makes an ostentatious pretension to wisdom; but simplicity of manners is the ally of integrity, and plain common sense is the main requisite of wisdom.

THE DOG INVITED TO SUPPER.

A Gentleman having invited several friends to supper, his Dog thought this a fit opportunity to invite another Dog, an intimate of his own, to partake with him of the good cheer, in the kitchen. Accordingly the stranger punctually attended, and seeing the mighty preparations going forward, promised himself a most delicious repast. He began to smell about, and, with his eyes intent upon the victuals, to lick his lips, and wag his tail. This drew the attention of the Cook, who stole slyly up, and seizing him by the hind legs, whirled him out of the window into the street. The Dog, stunned and hurt by his hard fall on the pavement, began to howl, the noise of which drew several Dogs about him, who knowing of the invitation, began to enquire how he had fared? O! charmingly, said he; only I ate and drank till I 'scarce knew which way I came out of the house.

APPLICATION.

THERE is no depending upon a second-hand interest; unless we know ourselves to be well with the principal, and are assured of his favour and protection, we stand upon a slippery foundation. They are strangers to the world who are so weak as to think they can be well with any one by proxy; they may by this means be cajoled, bubbled, and imposed upon, but are under great uncertainty as to gaining their point, and may probably be treated with scorn and derision in the end. Yet there are not wanting among the several species of fops, silly people of this sort, who pride themselves in an imaginary happiness, from being in the good graces of a great man's friend's friend. Alas! the great men themselves are but too apt to deceive and fail in making good their promises, how then can we expect any good from those who do but promise and vow in their names? To place a confidence in such sparks, is indeed so false a reliance, that we ought to be ashamed to be detected in it; and, like the Dog in the Fable, rather own we had been well treated, than let the world see how justly we had been punished for our ridiculous credulity.

THE ANGLER AND THE LITTLE FISH.

An Angler caught a small Trout, and as he was taking it off the hook, and going to put it into his basket, it opened its little throat, and begged most piteously that he would throw it into the river again. The man demanded what reason it had to expect this indulgence? Why, says the Fish, because I am so young and so little, that it is not worth your while taking me now, and certainly I shall be better worth your notice, if you take me a twelvemonth afterwards, when I shall be grown a great deal larger. That may be, replied the Angler, but I am sure of you now; and I am not one of those who quit a certainty in expectation of an uncertainty.

APPLICATION.

THEY who neglect the present opportunity of reaping a small advantage, in the hope that they shall obtain a greater afterwards, are far from acting upon a reasonable and well advised foundation. We ought never thus to deceive ourselves, and suffer the favourable moment to slip away; but secure to ourselves every fair advantage, however small, at the moment that it offers, without placing a vain reliance upon the visionary expectation of something better in time to come. Prudence advises us always to lay hold of time by the forelock, and to remember that "a bird in the hand is worth two in the bush."

A MAN BITTEN BY A DOG.

A Man, who had been sadly torn by a Dog, was advised by some Old Woman, as a cure, to dip a piece of bread in the wound, and give it to the Cur that bit him. He did so, and Æsop happening to pass by just at the time, asked him what he meant by it? The man informed him. Why then, says Æsop, do it as privately as you can, I beseech you; for if the rest of the Dogs of the town were to see you, we should all be eaten up alive by them.

APPLICATION.

VICE should always be considered as the proper object of punishment, and we should on no account connive at offences of an atrocious nature, much less

confer rewards on the criminals: for nothing contributes so much to the increase of roguery, as when
the undertakings of a knave are attended with success.
If it were not for the fear of punishment, a great part
of mankind, who now make a shift to keep themselves
honest, would be great villains.   But if criminals, instead of meeting with punishment, were, by having
been such, to attain honour and preferment, our natural inclination to mischief would be increased, and
we should be wicked out of emulation.   We should
rather strive to make virtue as tempting as possible,
and throw out every allurement in our power to draw
the minds of the wavering and unsettled to espouse
her cause.

THE FOX AND THE TIGER.

A skilful Archer coming into the woods, directed his arrows so successfully, that he slew many wild beasts, and wounded several others. This put the whole savage kind into a great consternation, and made them fly into the most retired thickets for refuge. At last, the Tiger resumed courage, and bidding them not be afraid, said that he alone would engage the enemy, telling them they might depend on his valour to avenge their wrongs. In the midst of these threats, while he was lashing himself with his tail, and tearing up the ground with anger, an arrow pierced his ribs, and hung by its barbed point in his side. He set up a loud and hideous roar, occasioned by the anguish he felt, and endeavoured to draw out the painful dart with his teeth: when the Fox approaching him, enquired with an air of surprise, who it was that could

Q 2

have strength and courage enough to wound so mighty
and valorous a beast? Ah! says the Tiger, I was
mistaken in my reckoning: it was that invincible Man
yonder.

APPLICATION.

THOUGH strength and courage are very good ingredients towards making us secure and formidable in the
world, yet unless there be a proper portion of wisdom
or policy to direct them, instead of being serviceable,
they often prove detrimental to their proprietors. A
rash forward man, who depends upon the excellence
of his own parts and accomplishments, is likewise apt
to expose a weak side, which his enemies might not
otherwise have observed; and gives an advantage to
others by those very means which he fancied might
have secured it to himself. Counsel and conduct always did and always will govern the world; and the
strong, in spite of all their force, can never avoid being tools to the crafty. Some men are as much superior to others in wisdom and policy, as man in general
is above the brute. Strength, ill-governed, opposed
to them, is like a quarter staff in the hands of a huge,
robust, but bungling fellow, who fights against a
master of the science. The latter, though without a
weapon, would have skill and address enough to disarm his adversary, and drub him with his own staff.
In a word, savage fierceness and brutal strength, must
not pretend to stand in competition with policy and
stratagem.

THE DOG AND THE SHADOW.

A Dog, crossing a rivulet with a piece of flesh in his mouth, saw his own shadow represented in the clear mirror of the stream; and believing it to be another Dog, who was carrying another piece of flesh, he could not forbear catching at it; but was so far from getting any thing by his greedy design, that he dropt the piece he had in his mouth, which immediately sunk to the bottom, and was irrecoverably lost.

APPLICATION.

Base is the man who pines amidst his store,
And fat with plenty, griping covets more.

Excessive greediness, in the end, mostly misses what it aims at, and he that catches at more than belongs

to him, justly deserves to lose what he has.   Yet nothing is more common, and, at the same time more
pernicious, than this selfish principle.   It prevails from
the king to the peasant; and all orders and degrees
of men are more or less infected with it.   Great monarchs have been drawn in by this greedy humour to
grasp at the dominions of their neighbours; not that
they wanted any thing more to feed their luxury, but
to gratify their insatiable appetite for vain glory; and
many states have been reduced to the last extremity
by attempting such unjust encroachments.   He that
thinks he sees the estate of another in a pack of cards,
or a box and dice, and ventures his own in the pursuit of it, should not repine, if he finds himself a
beggar in the end.

THE BEAR AND THE BEE-HIVES.

A Bear, climbing over the fence into a place where Bees were kept, began to plunder the hives, and rob them of their honey; but the Bees, to revenge the injury, attacked him in a whole swarm together; and though they were not able to pierce his rugged hide, yet, with their little stings they so annoyed his eyes and nostrils, that, unable to endure the smarting pain, with impatience he tore the skin over his ears, with his own claws, and suffered ample punishment for the injury he had done the Bees, in breaking open their waxen cells.

APPLICATION.

MANY and great are the injuries of which men are guilty towards each other, for the sake of gratifying some base appetite: for there are those who would not scruple to bring desolation upon their country, and run the hazard of their own necks into the bargain, rather than balk a wicked inclination, either of cruelty, ambition, or avarice. But it were to be wished, that all who are hurried on by such blind impulses, would consider a moment before they proceed to irrevocable execution. Injuries and wrongs not only call for revenge and reparation with the voice of equity itself, but oftentimes carry their punishment along with them; and, by an unforeseen train of events, are retorted on the head of the actor, who not seldom, from a deep remorse, expiates them upon himself by his own hand.

THE DRUNKEN HUSBAND.

A certain Woman had a Drunken Husband, whom she had endeavoured to reclaim by several ways, without effect. She, at last, tried this stratagem: when he was brought home one night dead drunk, she ordered him to be carried to a burial-place, and there laid in a vault, as if he had been dead indeed. Thus she left him, and went away till she thought he might be come to himself, and grown sober again. When she returned, and knocked at the door of the vault, the man cried out, who's there? I am the person, says she, in a dismal tone of voice, that waits upon the dead folks, and I am come to bring you some victuals. Ah, good waiter, says he, let the victuals alone and bring me a little drink, I beseech thee. The Woman hearing this, fell to tearing her hair, and beating her breast in a woeful manner: Unhappy wretch that I

am, says she, this was the only way that I could think
of to reform the beastly sot; but instead of gaining my
point, I am only convinced that his drunkenness is an
incurable habit, which he intends to carry with him
into the other world.

THIS Fable is intended to shew us the prevalence of
custom; and how by using ourselves to any evil practice, we may let it grow into such a habit as we shall
never be able to divest ourselves of. " O! that men
should put an enemy into their mouths to steal away
their brains!" There is no vice which gains an as-
cendant over us more insensibly, or more incurably,
than drunkenness: it takes root by degrees, and comes
at length to be past both remedy and shame. Habitual
drunkenness stupifies the senses, destroys the understanding, fills its votaries with diseases, and makes
them incapable of business. It cuts short the thread
of life, or brings on an early old age, besides the mischief it does in the mean time to a man's family and
affairs, and the scandal it brings upon himself: for a
sot is one of the most despicable and disgusting characters in life. After he has destroyed his reasoning
faculties, and thus shewn his ingratitude to the giver
of them, he flies to palliatives as a remedy for the diseases which his intemperance has caused, and goes on
in a course of taking whets and cordials, and more
drink, till he falls a martyr to the vice, to which
through life he has been a slave.

THE LIONESS AND THE FOX.

The Lioness and the Fox meeting together, fell into discourse, and the conversation turning upon the breeding and fruitfulness of some living creatures above others, the Fox could not forbear taking the opportunity of observing to the Lioness, that for her part, she thought Foxes were as happy in that respect as almost any other creatures; for they bred constantly once a year, if not oftener, and always had a good litter of cubs at every birth; and yet, says she, there are some folks who are never delivered of more than one at a time, and that perhaps not above once or twice in their whole lives, who hold up their noses, and value themselves so much upon it, that they think all other creatures beneath them, and scarce worthy to be spoken to. The Lioness, who all the time perceived at whom this reflection pointed, replied, what you have

observed is true.   You litter often, and produce a
great many at a time; but what are they? Foxes!
I, indeed, may have but one at a time; but you should
remember that that one is a Lion.

OUR productions, of whatsoever kind, are not to be
esteemed so much by their quantity as by their quality.
It is not being employed much, but well, and to the
purpose, which will make us useful to the age we live
in, and celebrated by those which are to come.   As the
multiplication of foxes and other vermin is a misfortune to the countries which are infested with them, so
one cannot help throwing out a melancholy reflection,
when one sees some particular classes of the human
kind increase so fast as they do.   But the most obvious
meaning of this Fable is the hint it gives us in relation
to authors.   These gentlemen should never attempt to
raise themselves a reputation by trumping up a long
catalogue of their various productions, since there is
more glory in having written one tolerable piece than
a thousand indifferent ones; and whoever has had the
good fortune to please in one literary performance,
should be very cautious how he stakes his reputation
in a second attempt.

THE LAMB BROUGHT UP BY A GOAT.

A Wolf, prowling about for his prey, espied a Lamb
sucking a Goat. You silly creature! says he, you quite
mistake; this is not your mother; she is yonder among
a flock of sheep: do allow me to conduct you to her.
No, no, replies the Lamb, the mother that bore me
may indeed be yonder; but when she dropped me, she
shewed no further care, but left me unprovided for,
to shift for myself, regardless of what might become of
me; and had it not been for the kindness of this honest
Goat, who took compassion upon my helplessness, I
must have suffered all the miseries to which inexperienced youth and innocence are exposed, when left
without a guide to the mercy of the world.

APPLICATION.

This Fable is levelled at those parents, too often met with in society, who, through negligence or ignorance of their duty, suffer their offspring to grow up to maturity, without instilling into their minds a single good principle of morality, or a reverence for religion, to guide them through life, and to guard them from falling into the snares of every wolf who may seek their destruction. Others again, more abandoned indeed, and callous to the tender ties of nature, bring forth an offspring whom they neither cherish nor provide for. Such a description of persons are not fit to become parents, and they must not be surprized, if their want of parental affection produce a corresponding want of filial attachment and respect: for the duties between parents and children are reciprocal. It is the goodness of parents which chiefly entitles them to the respect due to that name; and it is a paramount duty of children to honour, obey, and revere such parents as fulfil the obligations which the laws of God and nature impose upon those who bring children into the world.

THE HEN AND THE SWALLOW.

A Hen, having found a nest of Serpent's eggs in a dung-hill, immediately, with a fostering care, sat upon them, with a design to hatch them. A Swallow observing this, flew towards her, and with great earnestness forewarned her of her danger. What! said she, are you mad, to bring forth a brood of such pernicious creatures? Be assured, the instant they are warmed into life, you are the first they will attack and wreak their venomous spite upon: but the Hen persisted in her folly, and the end verified the Swallow's prediction.

APPLICATION.

It is too often the hard fortune of many a kind good-natured man in the world to breed up a bird to

pick out his own eyes, in despite of all cautions to the
contrary; but they who want foresight should hearken
to the council of the wise, as this might have the effect
of preventing their spending much time and good offices on the undeserving, perhaps to the utter ruin of
themselves.   It is the duty of all men to act fairly,
openly, and honestly, in all their transactions in life;
to do justice to all; but to consider well the character
of those on whom they would confer favours: for gratitude is one of the rarest as well as the greatest of
virtues.   The Fable is intended to shew that we should
never have any dealings with bad men, even to do
them kindnesses.   Men of evil principles are a gene-
ration of vipers, that ought to be crushed; and every
rogue should be looked upon by honest men as a venomous serpent.   The man who is occasionally, or by accident, one's enemy, may be mollified by kindness, and
reclaimed by good usage: such a behaviour both reason and morality expect from us: but we should ever
resolve, if not to suppress, at least to have no con-
nexion with those whose blood is tinctured with hereditary, habitual villainy, and their nature leavened with
evil, to such a degree as to be incapable of a reformation.

THE ENVIOUS MAN AND THE COVETOUS.

AN Envious Man happened to be offering up his prayers to Jupiter, at the same time and in the same place with a covetous miserable Fellow. Jupiter sent Apollo to examine the merits of their petitions, and to give them such relief as he should think proper. Apollo therefore opened his commission, and told them, that to make short of the matter, whatever the one asked, the other should have doubled. Upon this, the Covetous Man, who had a thousand things to request, forebore to ask first, hoping to receive a double quantity; for he concluded that all men's wishes sympathized with his own. By this circumstance, the Envious Man had the opportunity of giving vent to his malignity, and of preferring his petition first, which was what he aimed at; so without hesitation he prayed

S

to have one of his eyes put out, knowing that of consequence his companion would be deprived of both.

APPLICATION.

THIS Fable is levelled at two of the most odious passions which degrade the mind of man. In the extremes of their unsocial views, envy places its happiness in the misery and the misfortunes of others, and pines and sickens at their joy; and avarice, unblest amidst its stores, is never satisfied unless it can get all to itself, although its insatiable cravings are at once unaccountable, miserable, and absurd.

THE PORCUPINE AND THE SNAKES.

A Porcupine, wanting a shelter for himself, begged a nest of Snakes to give him admittance into their snug cave. They were prevailed upon, and let him in accordingly; but were so annoyed with his sharp prickly quills, that they soon repented of their easy compliance, and intreated the Porcupine to withdraw, and leave them their hole to themselves. No, said he, let them quit the place that dont like it; for my part, I am well enough satisfied as I am.

APPLICATION.

THIS Fable points out the danger of entering into any degree of friendship, alliance, or partnership with any person whatever, before we have thoroughly considered his nature and qualities, his circumstances, and his humour; and also the necessity of examining our own temper and disposition, to discover, if we can, how far these may accord with the genius of those with whom we are about to form a connection; otherwise our associations, of whatever kind they be, may prove the greatest plague of our life. Young people, who are warm in all their passions, and suffer them, like a veil, to hoodwink their reason, often throw open their arms at once, and admit into the greatest intimacy persons whom they know little of, but by false and uncertain lights, and thus, perhaps, take a Porcupine into their bosom, instead of an inmate who might sooth the cares of life, as an amiable consort, or a valuable friend.

THE SOW AND THE WOLF.

A Sow that had just farrowed, and lay in her sty with her whole litter of Pigs, was visited by a Wolf, who secretly longed to make a meal of one of them, but knew not how to come at it. So, under the pretence of a friendly visit, he gave her a call, and endeavoured to insinuate himself into her good graces by his apparently kind enquiries after the welfare of herself and her young family. Can I be of any service to you, Mrs Sow? said he: if I can, it shall not on my part be wanting; and if you have a mind to go abroad for a little fresh air, you may depend upon my taking as much care of your young family as you could do yourself. No, I thank you, Mr Wolf, I thoroughly understand your meaning, and the greatest favour you can do to me and my Pigs, is to keep your distance.

APPLICATION.

WHEN an entire stranger, or any one of whom we
have no reason to entertain a good opinion, obtrudes
upon us an offer of his services, we ought to look to
our own safety, and shew a shyness and coldness towards him.   But there are also many men with whom
it is dangerous to have the least connection, and with
whom any commerce or correspondence will certainly be to our detriment.   From these we should,
therefore, resolve not to accept even favours, but carefully avoid being under any obligation to them: for
in the end, their apparent kindness will shew itself to
be a real injury; and there is no method of guarding
so effectually against such people, as that of entirely
avoiding their society, or shutting our doors against
them, as we would do against a thief.

THE FROGS AND THEIR KING.

In antient times, the nation of Frogs lived an easy free life among their lakes and ponds; but at length grew dissatisfied with such a continuance of undisturbed tranquillity, and petitioned Jupiter for a king. Jupiter smiled at their folly, and threw them down a log of wood, and with a thundering voice said, " there is a king for you." With this, and the sudden splash it made in the water, they were at first quite panic-struck, and for some time durst not put their heads up; but by degrees they ventured to take a peep, and at length even to leap upon the log. Not being pleased with so tame and insipid a king, they again petitioned Jupiter for another, who would exert more authority. Jupiter, disgusted at their importunate folly, sent them a Stork for their king, who, without ceremony, eat them up whenever his craving appetite required a supply.

APPLICATION.

THIS Fable is said to have been spoken by Æsop
to the Athenians, who had flourished under their commonwealth, and lived under good and wholesome laws
of their own enacting, until, in process of time, they
suffered their liberty to run into licentiousness; and
factious designing men fomented divisions, and raised
animosities among them. When thus rendered weak,
Pisistratus took the advantage, and seized upon their
citadel and liberties both together. The Athenians
finding themselves in a state of slavery, though their
tyrant happened to be a merciful one, could not bear
the thoughts of it; but Æsop in reciting the Fable to
them, prescribes patience where there was no other remedy, and adds, at last, " Wherefore, my dear coun-
trymen, be contented with your present condition, bad
as it is, for fear a change should make it worse."

Set them up with a King indeed!

THE OLD WOMAN AND THE EMPTY CASK.

An Old Woman, seeing a Wine Cask, which had been emptied of its contents, but the very lees of which still perfumed the air with a grateful cordial scent, applied her nose to the bunghole, and snuffing very heartily for some time, at last broke out into this exclamation: O delicious smell! How good! how charming must you have been once, when your very dregs are so agreeable and refreshing!

APPLICATION.

Phædrus was an old man when he wrote his Fables, and this he applies to himself; intimating what we ought to judge of his youth, when his old age was capable of such productions. It is at once a pleasing and

T

melancholy idea that is given us by the intercourse
with elderly persons, whose conversation is relishing
and agreeable, and we cannot help concluding that
they must have been very engaging in the prime of life,
when in their decline they are still capable of yielding
us so much pleasure. Nor can we help feeling regret,
that this fountain of delight is now almost dried up,
and going to forsake us for ever. On the contrary,
when people have neglected to cultivate their minds in
youth, their whole deportment through life is marked
with the effects of this great want, and their old age is
burthensome to themselves, and their conversation insipid to others; and like liquor of a thin body, and
vile quality, soon becomes sour, vapid, or good for
nothing.

an old filtering stone

JUPITER AND THE CAMEL.

THE Camel presented a petition to Jupiter, complaining of the hardships of his case, in not having, like bulls and other creatures, horns, or any weapon of defence to protect himself from the attacks of his enemies; and praying that relief might be granted him in such manner as should be thought most expedient. Jupiter could not help smiling at his impertinent address; but, however, rejected the petition, and told him, that so far from granting his unreasonable request, he would take care that henceforward his ears should be shortened, as a punishment for his presumptuous importunity.

APPLICATION.

THE nature of things is so fixed in every particular,

T 2

that they are very weak, superstitious people, who
think that it can be altered.   But besides the impos-
sibility of producing a change by foolish importunities,
they who employ much of their time in that way, instead of getting, are sure to lose in the end.   When
any man is so silly and vexatious as to make unreasonable complaints, and to harbour undue repinings in his
heart, his peevishness will lessen the real good which
he possesses, and the sourness of his temper shorten
that allowance of comfort which he already thinks too
scanty.   Thus, in truth, it is not Providence, but ourselves, who punish our own importunity, in soliciting
for impossibilities, with a sharp corroding care, which
abridges us of some part of that little pleasure which
Heaven has cast into our lot.

> Happy the man without a wish for more,
> Who quietly enjoys his little store,
> And knows to heaven, with gratitude to pay
> Thanks for what's given, and what is ta'en away.

THE STAG AND THE FAWN.

A Stag, grown old and mischievous, was, according to custom, stamping with his foot, making threatening motions with his head, and bellowing so terribly, that the whole herd quaked for fear of him; when one of the little Fawns coming up, addressed him to this purpose: Pray what is the reason that you, who are so stout and formidable at all other times, if you do but hear the cry of the hounds, are ready to fly out of your skin for fear? What you observe is true, replied the Stag, though I know not how to account for it: I am indeed vigorous and able enough, I think, to defend myself against all attacks, and often resolve with myself, that nothing shall ever dismay my courage for the future; but, alas! I no sooner hear the voice of the hounds, but all my spirits fail, and I cannot help making off as fast as my legs can carry me.

APPLICATION.

Try what we can, do what we will,
Yet nature will be nature still.

THE predominance of nature will generally shew itself through all the disguises which artful men endeavour to throw over it. Cowardice particularly gives us but the more suspicion of its existence, when it would conceal itself under an affected fierceness, as they who would smother an ill smell by a cloud of perfume, are imagined to be but the more offensive. When we have done all, nature will remain what she was, and shew herself whenever she is called upon: therefore, whatever we do in contradiction to her laws, is so forced and affected, that it must needs expose and make us truly ridiculous.

THE FIR AND THE BRAMBLE.

A tall Fir, that stood towering up in the forest, was so proud of his dignity and high station, that he looked with disdain upon the little shrubs that grew beneath him. A lowly Bramble had often been made to feel the insults and gloomy frowns of his lofty neighbour, who, on the slightest rufflings of the winds, shook his extended arms over the humble shrub, and upbraided him with his contemptible situation. As for me, said the Fir, I am the first in the forest for beauty and rank: my top shoots up into the clouds, and my branches display a perpetual verdure, whilst you lie grovelling upon the ground, and could not live were I to leave off sprinkling you with the drops from my extremities. At this the Bramble set up his prickles, and replied, that this haughtiness arose from pride and ignorance; for He that made thee a lofty tree, could,

with equal ease, have made thee an humble Bramble;
and high as thou art, a puff of His breath, in the mes-
sage of a north wind, can rob thee of thy verdure, or
lay thee low; and further, I pray thee tell me, when
the woodman comes with his axe to fell timber, whether thou wouldst not rather be a Bramble than a Fir?

APPLICATION.

PRIDE, which was implanted in the human breast
for wise purposes, should carefully be directed aright.
It was intended only to exalt the minds of all ranks
and conditions of men, to that pitch, which will make
them spurn at, and despise the doing of a mean or dishonourable action; and it is only misapplied, when it
puffs up those whom fortune has placed in high stations, or overloaded with riches, and tempts them to
look down with derision on those below them.   The
higher a man is exalted in life, but especially if he have
risen by dishonourable means, the more unlikely it is
that he will escape a storm, or the mischiefs to which
he may be exposed in his public capacity, in any con-
vulsion that may befal his country.   When public justice overtakes him, and he finds the day of reckoning
near at hand, the honest monitor within will put him
in mind of his true situation, and he will then be enabled to make a just comparison between his own lofty
station, and that of the poor, but honest, man.

THE BEES, THE DRONES, AND THE WASP.

A number of Drones, who had long lived at their ease in a hive of Bees, without contributing by their labour to make any honey, at length began to dispute the right of the Bees, and insisted that both the honey and the combs were their property. The Bees, after much altercation, at last offered to leave the dispute to reference, and this being assented to by the Drones, the Wasp was chosen umpire. Accordingly, he began by declaring, that as both parties, he hoped, were his friends, and he wished them well, he would instantly proceed upon the investigation. I must own, says he, that the point is somewhat dubious, for I have often seen you both in the same hive, and excepting that the Drones are of a more

U

portly size and appearance, you are all otherwise nearly alike in person: but as I have not been able to see
who worked, and who did not, I know of no mode
in which I shall be enabled to judge so correctly, as
by setting each party to work at the making of the
honey. Therefore, addressing himself to the Bees,
you take one hive; and you, speaking to the Drones,
will be so good as to take another, and both go to
work to make honey as fast as you can. The Bees
readily accepted the proposal; but the Drones hung
back, and would not agree to it. So, so! says Judge
Wasp, I see clearly how the matter stands; and without further ceremony, declared in favour of the Bees.

APPLICATION.

The surest method of detecting ignorance and inability, is to put arrogant pretenders to the test, and
appreciate their claims by a fair trial; and when those
who assume the merit due to works of ingenuity, refuse
to prove their title by a display of their talents, we may
well conclude that their pretensions are unfounded, and
that they are mere impostors. When men, who are at
the head of national affairs, will not be at the pains to
find out merit (for men of that character are too modest
to obtrude themselves) they will be surrounded by a
swarm of idle, impudent, good-for-nothing drones;
and these too often succeed in obtaining those benefits
which should be the reward of men of parts, integrity, and industry.

THE FROG AND THE FOX.

A Frog leaping out of the lake, and taking the advantage of a rising ground, made a proclamation to all the beasts of the forest, that he was an able physician, and for curing all manner of distempers, would turn his back to no person living. This discourse, with the aid of some hard cramp words, which nobody understood, made the beasts admire his learning, and give credit to every thing he said. At last, the Fox, who was present, with indignation asked him, how he could have the impudence, with those thin lanthorn jaws, that meagre pale phiz, and blotched spotted body, to pretend to cure the infirmities of others?

APPLICATION.

A sickly and infirm look is as disadvantageous in a

physician, as a rakish one in a clergyman, or a sheepish one in a soldier.　We should not set up for correctors of the faults of others, whilst we labour under the same ourselves.　Good advice ought always to be followed, without our being prejudiced upon account of the person from whom it comes; but it is seldom that men can be brought to think us worth minding, when we prescribe cures for maladies with which we ourselves are afflicted.　Physician heal thyself, is too scriptural, not to be applied upon such an occasion; and if we would avoid being the jest of an audience, we must be sound and free from those diseases of which we would endeavour to cure others.　How shocked must people have been to hear a preacher for a whole hour declaim against drunkenness, when his own weaknesses have been such, that he could neither bear nor forbear drinking, and perhaps was the only person in the congregation who made the doctrine at that time necessary!　Others, too, have been very zealous in censuring crimes, of which none were suspected more than themselves: but let such silly hypocrites remember, that they whose eyes want couching, are the most improper people in the world to set up for oculists.

THE CAT AND THE MICE.

A certain house being much infested with Mice, a Cat was at length procured, who very diligently hunted after them, and killed great numbers every night. The Mice, being exceedingly alarmed at this destruction among their family, consulted together upon what was best to be done for their preservation against so terrible and cruel an enemy. After some debate, they came to the resolution, that no one should, in future, descend below the uppermost shelf. The Cat, observing their extreme caution, endeavoured to draw them down to their old haunts by stratagem, for which purpose, she suspended herself by her hinder legs upon a peg in the pantry, and hoped by this trick to lull their suspicions, and to entice them to venture within her reach. She had not long been in this posture, before a cunning old Mouse peeped over the

edge of the shelf, and squeaked out thus: Aha ! Mrs
Puss, are you there then ?   There may you be; but I
would not trust myself with you, though your skin
were stuffed with straw.

APPLICATION.

WE cannot be too much upon our guard against
fraud and imposition of every kind; and prudence in
many cases would rather counsel us to forego some advantages, than endeavour to gain them at a risk of
which we cannot certainly ascertain the amount. We
should more particularly suspect some design in the
professions of those who have once injured us; and
though they may promise fairly for the future, it is no
breach of charity to doubt their sincerity, and decline
their proposals, however plausible they may appear ;
for experience shews that many of the misfortunes
which we experience through life, are caused by our
own too great credulity.

THE OAK AND THE REED.

An Oak, which hung over the bank of a river, was blown down by a violent storm of wind, and as it was carried along by the stream, some of its boughs brushed against a Reed which grew near the shore. This struck the Oak with a thought of admiration, and he could not forbear asking the Reed how he came to stand so secure and unhurt, in a tempest which had been furious enough to tear up an Oak by the roots? Why, says the Reed, I secure myself by a conduct the reverse of yours: instead of being stubborn and stiff, and confiding in my strength, I yield and bend to the blast, and let it go over me, knowing how vain and fruitless it would be to resist.

APPLICATION.

Though a tame submission to injuries which it is in

our power to redress, be generally esteemed a base and dishonourable thing, yet to resist where there is no probability, or even hope of getting the better, may also be looked upon as the effect of a blind temerity, and perhaps of a weak understanding. The strokes of fortune are oftentimes as irresistible as they are severe, and he who with an impatient spirit fights against her, instead of alleviating, does but double the blows upon himself. A person of a quiet still temper, whether it be given him by nature, or acquired by art, calmly composes himself in the midst of a storm, so as to elude the shock, or receive it with the least detriment,—like a prudent experienced sailor, who, in swimming to the shore from a wrecked vessel, in a swelling sea, does not oppose the fury of the waves, but stoops and gives way, that they may roll over his head without obstruction. The doctrine of absolute submission in all cases, is an absurd dogmatical precept, with nothing but ignorance and superstition to support it; but, upon particular occasions, and where it is impossible for us to overcome, to submit patiently is one of the most reasonable maxims of life.

O God of infinite Wisdom Truth Justice & Mercy I thank Thee

FORTUNE AND THE BOY.

A School Boy, fatigued with play, laid himself down by the brink of a deep well, where he fell fast asleep. Fortune, whose wheel is always in motion, passing by, kindly gave him a tap on the head, and awoke him. My good boy, said she, arise and depart from this dangerous situation immediately; for if you had tumbled into this well, and been drowned, your friends would not have attributed the accident to your carelessness, but would have laid the whole blame upon me.

APPLICATION.

MANKIND suffer more evils from their own imprudence, than from events which it is not in their power to controul; but they are ever ready to complain of the

x

perverseness of chance, and the capriciousness of fortune, and to impute the blame to her for whatever mischiefs may befal them, when these clearly arise from their own misconduct.   Few men pass through life without having had reason at one time or another to thank Fortune for her favours; and great is the number of those who have, through their own folly, indolence, or inattention, neglected to profit by her kindness. Prudent people take every care not to put themselves in the power of accidents; but those who carelessly give up all their concerns to the guidance of blind chance, must not be surprised if by some of the revolutions of Fortune's wheel, they feel the punishment due to their negligence and folly.

The Butchers Coat of arms

THE WOLF AND THE CRANE.

A Wolf, after devouring his prey, happened to have a bone stick in his throat, which gave him so much pain, that he went howling up and down, and importuning every creature he met to lend him a kind hand in order to his relief; nay, he promised a reasonable reward to any one who should perform the operation with success. At last, the Crane undertook the business, ventured his long neck into the rapacious felon's throat, plucked out the bone, and asked for the promised reward. The Wolf, turning his eyes disdainfully towards him, said, I did not think you had been so unconscionable: I had your head in my mouth, and could have bit it off whenever I pleased, but suffered you to take it away without any damage, and yet you are not contented !

x 2

Who serves a villain, might as wisely free
The hardened murderer from the fatal tree.

APPLICATION.

THERE are people in the world to whom it may be
wrong to do services, upon a double score: first, because they never deserve to have a good office done
them; and secondly, because when once engaged, it is
so hard a matter to get well rid of their acquaintance.
We ought to consider what kind of people they are,
to whom we are desired to do good offices, before we
do them: for he that grants a favour, or even confides
in a person of no honour, instead of finding his account
in it, comes off well, if he be no sufferer in the end.

THE HART AND THE VINE.

A Hart being closely pursued by the Hunters, concealed himself under the broad leaves of a shady Vine.
When the Hunters were gone by, and had given him
over for lost, he thinking himself very secure, began
to crop and eat the leaves of his shelter. By this, the
branches being put into a rustling motion drew the attention of some of the Hunters that way, who seeing
the Vine stir, and fancying some wild beast had taken
covert there, shot their arrows at a venture, and killed
the Deer. Before he expired, he uttered his dying
words to this purpose: " Ah!" says he, " I suffer
justly for my ingratitude; because I could not forbear
doing an injury to the Vine, which so kindly concealed
me in time of danger."

APPLICATION.

THERE is no maxim which deserves more frequent repetition, and if the heart be capable of amendment by precept and admonition, no virtue should be more strongly enforced and recommended than gratitude. Where sentiments of this kind are wanting, our natures soon become debased, and our minds depraved. Ingratitude has ever been justly branded as the blackest of crimes, and, as it were, comprehending all other vices within it. Nor can we say that this opinion is too severe: for if a man be capable of injuring his benefactor, what will he scruple doing towards another? We may fairly conclude that he who is guilty of ingratitude, will not hesitate at any other crime of an inferior nature. Since there are no human laws to punish this infamous prevailing vice, it would only be doing an act of justice, and supplying the want, to point out criminals of this description to the reprobation of mankind, that men of worth might avoid all intercourse and communication with them. The ingrate should also bear in mind, that he strips himself of the protection which might have been afforded by his friends, and exposes himself to the shafts of his enemies, who will not fail to take advantage of the defenceless state to which his folly and depravity have reduced him.

THE HUNTED BEAVER.

A Beaver, having strayed far from his dwelling, (which it is well known these animals construct with infinite sagacity) was closely pursued by the hunters, and knowing that he was thus persecuted for the sake of the castor, which is contained in two little bags placed underneath and near the tail, he, with great resolution and presence of mind, bit them off with his teeth, and leaving them behind him, thus escaped with his life.

APPLICATION.

It is in vain for individuals to contend against an overwhelming power, and an ineffectual resistance to violence only tends to double our sufferings. When life is pursued, and in danger, whoever values it should give up every thing but his honour to preserve it; and there can be no disgrace in yielding voluntarily to our persecutors, when we are certain that resistance is in vain: but this doctrine can seldom be applied to the case of a whole nation, for when tyranny and rapine are making their wicked strides over a country (as has sometimes happened even in Europe) the people would seldom fail to rid themselves of their oppressors, if they resolved to rise as one man, and bravely oppose them.

THE ASS AND THE LION HUNTING.

THE Lion, having thinned the forest of great numbers of the beasts upon which he preyed, and so scared and intimidated the rest, that he found it very difficult to get hold of any more of them, bethought himself of a new expedient to obtain more readily a fresh supply. He invited the Ass to assist him in his plan, and gave him instructions how to act. Go, said the Lion, and hide thyself in yonder thicket, and then let me hear thee bray in the most frightful manner thou possibly canst. The stratagem took effect accordingly. The Ass brayed most hideously, and the timorous beasts, not knowing what to think of it, began to scour off as fast as they could; when the Lion, who was posted at a proper avenue, seized and killed them as he pleased. Having got his belly full, he called out to the Ass, and bade him leave off, telling him he had done enough.

Y

Upon this, the long-eared brute came out of his ambush, and approaching the Lion, asked him, with an air of conceit, how he liked his performance? Prodigiously! says he, you did it so well, that I protest had I not known your nature and temper, I might have been frightened myself.

APPLICATION.

A bragging cowardly fellow may impose upon people that do not know him; but is the greatest jest imaginable to those who do. There are many men who appear very terrible and big in their manner of expressing themselves, and if you could be persuaded to take their own word for it, are perfect Lions; but if we take the pains to enquire a little into their true nature, are as arrant Asses as ever brayed.

THE SOW AND THE BITCH.

A Sow and a Bitch happening to meet, a debate arose between them concerning their fruitfulness. The Bitch insisted upon it, that she brought forth more at a litter, and oftener, than any other four-legged creature. Nay, said the Sow, you do not do so, for others are as prolific as you; and besides, you are always in such a hurry, that you bring your puppies into the world blind.

APPLICATION.

It is no wonder that our productions should come into the world blind or lame, or otherwise defective, when by forced or unnatural methods we accelerate their birth, and impatiently refuse to let them go their full time. Then it is that the excellent proverb of the more haste the worse speed, is felt and fully verified. This Fable has been pointed at those authors whose itch for scribbling has been an annoyance to the world, rather than of any real use to it; and who have been proud of, and boasted of the numerous but flimsy productions of their vain and shallow brains. It is proper to put such people in mind, that it is not he who does most, but he who does the best, that will meet the approbation of mankind.

who told the Lamb to suck its mothers Paps?

THE SATYR AND THE TRAVELLER.

A Satyr, as he was ranging the forest in an exceeding cold snowy season, met with a Traveller half-starved with the extremity of the weather. He took compassion on him, and kindly invited him home to a warm cave he had in the hollow of a rock. As soon as they had entered and sat down, notwithstanding there was a good fire in the place, the chilly Traveller could not forbear blowing his fingers. Upon the Satyr asking him why he did so? He answered, that he did it to warm his hands. The honest Sylvan having seen little of the world, admired a man who was master of so valuable a quality as that of blowing heat; and therefore resolved to entertain him in the best manner he could. He spread the table with dried fruits of several sorts, and produced a remnant of old cordial wine, which he mulled with some warm spices over the fire, and presented to his shivering guest. But this the Traveller thought fit to blow upon likewise; and when the Satyr demanded a reason why he did so, he replied, to cool his dish. This second answer provoked the Satyr's indignation as much as the first had kindled his surprise; so, taking the man by the shoulders, he thrust him out of the place, saying, he would have nothing to do with a wretch who had so vile a quality as to blow hot and cold with the same breath.

APPLICATION.

NOTHING can be more offensive to a man of a sincere honest heart, than he who blows with different breaths from the same mouth: who flatters a man to his face, and reviles him behind his back. Such double-dealing false friends ought and will always be considered as unworthy of being treated otherwise than as worthless and disagreeable persons: for unless the tenor of a man's life be always true and consistent with itself, the less one has to do with him the better. It is unfortunately too common with persons of this cast of character, in the exalted stations of life, to serve a present view, or perhaps only the caprice or whim of the moment, to blow nothing but what is warm, benevolent, and cherishing, to raise up the expectations of a dependent to the highest degree; and when they suspect he may prove troublesome, they then, by a sudden cold forbidding air, easily blast all his hopes and expectations: but such a temper, whether it proceed from a designed or natural levity, is detestable, and has been the cause of much trouble and mortification to many a brave deserving man.

THE FOX AND THE GRAPES.

A hungry Fox coming into a vineyard where there hung delicious clusters of ripe Grapes, his mouth watered to be at them; but they were nailed up to a trellis so high, that with all his springing and leaping he could not reach a single bunch. At last, growing tired and disappointed, Let who will take them! says he, they are but green and sour; so I'll e'en let them alone.

APPLICATION.

To affect to despise that which they have long ineffectually laboured to obtain, is the only consolation to which weak minds can have recourse, both to palliate their inability, and to take off the bitterness of disappointment. There is a strange propensity in mankind to this temper, and there is a numerous class of vain coxcombs in the world, who, because they would never be thought to be disappointed in any of their pursuits, pretend a dislike to every thing they cannot obtain. The discarded statesman, considering the corruption of the times, would not have any hand in the administration of affairs for the world! The needy adventurer, and pretended patriot, would fain persuade all who will listen to them, that they would not go cringing and creeping into a drawing-room, for the best place the king has in his disposal! Worthless young fellows, who find that their addresses to virtue and beauty are rejected; and poor rogues who laugh to scorn the rich and great, are all alike in saying, like sly Reynard, the Grapes are sour!

THE MISCHIEVOUS DOG.

A certain Man had a Dog which was so ferocious and surly, that he was compelled to fasten a heavy clog to his collar, to keep him from running at and indiscriminately seizing upon every animal that came in his way. This the vain Cur took for a badge of honourable distinction, and grew so insolent upon it, that he looked down with an air of scorn upon the neighbouring Dogs, and refused to keep them company: but a sly old poacher, who was one of the gang, assured him that he had no reason to value himself upon the favour he wore, since it was fixed upon him as a badge of disgrace, not of honour.

APPLICATION.

THE only true way of estimating the value of tokens

z

of distinction, is to reflect on what account they were
conferred. Those which have been acquired for virtuous actions, will be regarded as illustrious signs of
dignity; but if they have been bestowed upon the
worthless and base, as the reward of vice or corruption, all the stars and garters, and collars of an illustrious order,—all the tinsel glories in which such creatures may strut about in fancied superiority, will not
mask them from the sight of men of discernment, who
will always consider the means by which their honours
have been obtained, and truly estimate them as badges
of abasement and disgrace.

THE BULL AND THE GOAT.

A Bull being pursued by a Lion, fled towards a cave, in which he designed to secure himself; but was opposed at the entrance by a Goat, who had got possession before him, and, threatening a kind of defiance with his horns, seemed resolved to dispute the pass. The Bull, who thought he had no time to lose in a contest of this nature, immediately made off; but told the Goat, that it was not for fear of him or his defiances: for, says he, if the Lion were not so near, I would soon teach you the difference between a Bull and a Goat.

APPLICATION.

O'er-match'd, unaided, and his foes at hand,
Safely the coward may the brave withstand;
But think not, dastard, thus thy glories shine—
He fears a greater force, but scoffs at thine.

IT is very inhuman to deny succour and comfort to
people in tribulation; but to insult them, and add to
their misfortunes, is something superlatively brutish and
cruel.   There is, however, in the world, a sort of people of this vile temper, and littleness of mind, who
wait for an opportunity of aggravating their neighbour's affliction, and defer the execution of their evil
inclinations until they can do it with the severest effect.
If a person suffer under an expensive law-suit, lest he
should escape from that, one of these gentlemen will
take care to arrest him in a second action, hoping, at
least, to keep him at bay, while the more powerful
adversary attacks him on the other side.   One cannot
consider this temper, without observing something re-
markably cowardly in it: for these shuffling antagonists
never begin their encounter till they are very sure the
person they aim at is already over-matched.

THE FISHERMAN.

A certain Fisherman having laid his nets in the river, and placed them across the whole stream from one side to the other, took a long pole, and fell to beating the water to make the fish strike into his nets. One of his neighbours seeing him do so, wondered what he meant, and going up to him, Friend, says he, what are you doing here? Do you think it is to be suffered that you shall stand splashing and dashing the water, and making it so muddy, that it is not fit for use? Who do you think can live at this rate? He was going on in a great fury, when the other interrupted him, and replied, I do not much trouble myself how you are to live with my doing this; but I assure you I cannot live without it.

APPLICATION.

This Fable is levelled at those who love to " fish in troubled waters," and whose execrable principles are such, that they care not what mischief or what confusion they occasion in the world, provided they can obtain their ends, or even gratify some little selfish appetite. Little villains would set fire to a town, provided they could rake something of value to themselves out of its ashes; or kindle the flames of discord among friends and neighbours, purely to gratify their own malicious temper; and among the great ones there are those who, to succeed in their ambitious designs, will make no scruple of involving their country in divisions and animosities at home, and sometimes in war and bloodshed abroad: provided they do but maintain themselves in power, they care not what havoc and desolation they bring upon the rest of mankind. Their only reason is, that it must be so, because they cannot live as they wish without it. But brutish unsocial sentiments like these, are such as a mere state of nature would scarcely suggest; and it is perverting the very end, and overturning the first principles of society, when, instead of contributing to the welfare of mankind, in return for the benefits we receive from them, we thrive by their misfortunes, or subsist by their ruin. Those, therefore, who have the happiness of mankind at heart, (for happiness and morality are inseparably connected) should enter their protest against such wicked selfish notions, and oppose them with all their might; at the same time shunning the society of their possessors as a plague, and consigning their characters to the detestation of posterity.

THE FOX AND THE BOAR.

THE Fox, in traversing the forest, observed a Boar rubbing his tusks against a tree. Why how now, said the Fox, why make those martial preparations of whetting the teeth, since there is no enemy near that I can perceive? That may be, said the Boar; but you ought to know, Master Reynard, that we should scour up our arms while we have leisure: for in time of danger we shall have something else to do; and it is a good thing always to be prepared against the worst that can happen.

APPLICATION.

ALL business that is necessary to be done should be done betimes: for there is as little trouble in doing it in season as out of season; and he that is always ready

can never be taken by surprize.   Wise, just, and vigilant governments know that they cannot be safe in
peace, unless they are always prepared for war, and
are ready to meet the worst that can happen.   When
they become corrupt, or supine, and off their guard,
they thereby invite and expose their country to the
sudden attacks of its enemies.   In private life, many
evils and calamities befal those who make no provision
against unforeseen or untoward accidents, which the
prudent man prevents by looking forward to proba-
ble contingencies, and having a reserve of every thing
necessary before-hand,—that he may not be put into
hurry and confusion, nor thrown into dilemmas and
difficulties, when the time comes that he may have to
encounter them.   It cannot be too strongly impressed
upon the minds of all men, that day by day they are
approaching towards old age, and that they should
honourably endeavour to provide a store of conveniences against that time, when they will be most in
want of them, and least able to procure them.   To
reflect properly upon this, will give them pleasure instead of pain ; and they will not die a day sooner for
being always ready for that certain event : to do otherwise is acting like weak-minded men, who delay making their wills, and properly settling their worldly
affairs, because to them it looks so like the near approach of death.

CÆSAR AND THE SLAVE.

As Tiberius Cæsar was upon a journey to Naples, he stopped at a house which he had upon the mountain Misenus. As he was walking in the gardens attached to the house, one of his domestic slaves appeared in the walks, sprinkling the ground with a watering pot, in order to lay the dust, and this he did so officiously, and ran with so much alertness from one walk to another, that wherever the Emperor went, he still found this fellow mighty busy with his watering pot. But at last his design being discovered, which was to attract the notice of Cæsar by his extraordinary diligence, in the hope that he would make him free,—part of the ceremony of doing which consisted in giving the Slave a gentle stroke on one side of his face,—his imperial Majesty being disposed to be merry, called the Man to

2 A

him, and when he came up, full of the joyful expectation of his liberty, Hark you friend, says he, I have
observed that you have been very busy a great while;
but you were officiously meddling where you had nothing to do, while you might have employed your time
better elsewhere; and therefore I must tell you, that
I cannot afford a box on the ear at so low a price as
you bid for it.

APPLICATION.

PHÆDRUS tells us upon his word, that this is a true
story, and that he wrote it for the sake of a set of industrious idle gentlemen at Rome, who were harassed
and fatigued with a daily succession of care and trouble, because they had nothing to do. Always in a
hurry, but without business; busy, but to no purpose;
labouring under a voluntary necessity, and taking
abundance of pains to shew they were good for nothing. But what great town or city is so entirely free
of this sect, as to render the moral of this Fable useless any where? For it points at all those officious good-
natured people, who are eternally running up and
down to serve their friends, without doing them any
good; who, by a complaisance wrong judged or ill applied, displease whilst they endeavour to oblige, and
are never doing less to the purpose than when they are
most employed. In a word, this Fable is designed for
the reformation of all those who endeavour to gain for
themselves benefits and applause, from a misapplied
industry. It is not our being busy and officious that
will procure us the esteem of men of sense; but the
application of our actions to some noble useful purpose, and for the general good of mankind.

THE FROGS AND THE FIGHTING BULLS.

A Frog, one day, peeping out of the lake, and looking about him, saw two Bulls fighting at some distance
off in the meadow, and calling to his associates, Look,
says he, what dreadful work is yonder! Dear sirs,
what will become of us? Tush, said one of his companions, do not frighten yourself so about nothing;
how can their quarrels affect us? They are of a different kind, and are at present only contending which
shall be master of the herd. That is true, replies the
first, their quality and station in life are different from
ours; but as one of them will certainly prove conqueror,
he that is worsted, being beaten out of the meadow,
will take refuge here in the marshes, and possibly tread
some of us to death; so you see we are more nearly
concerned in this dispute of theirs, than you were at
first aware.

APPLICATION.

A wise man, however low his condition in life, looks forward through the proper and natural course and connection of causes and effects; and in so doing, he fortifies his mind against the worst that can befal him. It is of no small importance to the honest and quiet part of mankind, who desire nothing so much as to see peace and virtue flourish, to consider well the consequences that may arise to them out of the quarrels and feuds of the great, and to endeavour, by every means in their power, to avoid being in any way drawn in by their influence to become a party concerned in their broils and disputes: for no matter in which way the strife between the high contending parties may terminate, those who may have had the misfortune to be concerned with them, ought to think themselves well off if they do not smart for it severely in the end. How often has it happened, that men in eminent stations, who want to engross all power into their own hands, begin, under the mask of patriotism, to foment divisions and form factions, and excite animosities between well-meaning, but undiscerning people, without whose aid in one way or another they could not succeed; but who, at the same time, little think that the great aim of their leaders is nothing more than the advancement of their own private interest, or ambitious ends. The good of the public is always pretended upon such occasions, and may sometimes happen to be tacked to their own; but then it is purely accidental, and never was originally intended.

THE OLD HOUND.

An Old Hound, who had excelled in his time, and given his Master great satisfaction in many a chace, at last, through age, became feeble and unserviceable. However, being in the field one day, when the Stag was almost run down, he happened to be the first that came in with him, and seized him by the haunch; but his decayed and broken teeth not being able to keep their hold, the Deer escaped; upon which, his Master fell into a great passion, and began to whip him severely. The honest old creature is said to have barked out this apology: Ah! do not thus strike your poor old servant: it is not my heart and inclination, but my strength and speed, that fail me. If what I now am displease you, pray do not forget what I have been!

APPLICATION.

O let not those, whom honest servants bless,
With cruel hands their age infirm oppress;
Forget their service past, their former truth,
And all the cares and labours of their youth.

THIS Fable is intended to reprove the ingratitude
too common among mankind, which leaves the faithful
servant to want and wretchedness, after he has spent
the prime of his life in our service for a bare subsistence.   Where slavery is allowed, the laws compel the
master to provide for the worn-out slave; and where
there is no law to enforce the debt of gratitude, none
but those who are insensible to all the finer feelings of
humanity will neglect it.   Those who forget past services, and treat their faithful servants or friends unkindly or injuriously, when they are no longer of use
to them, however high their pride, are unworthy of
the name of gentleman.   They are, indeed, commonly
of an upstart breed, with whom the failure of human
nature itself is imputed as a crime; and servants and
dependents, instead of being considered their fellow-
men, are treated like brutes for not being more than
men.   The imprudence of this conduct is equal to its
wickedness, inasmuch as it directly tends to extinguish
the honest desire to please and to act faithfully, in the
younger servants, when they see that worn-out merit
thus goes unrewarded.   Humanity and gratitude are
the greatest ornaments of the human mind, and when
they are extinguished, every generous and noble sentiment perishes along with them.

THE TWO BITCHES.

A Bitch, who was just ready to whelp, intreated another to lend her her kennel only till her month was up, and assured her that then she should have it again. The other very readily consented, and with a great deal of civility, resigned it to her immediately. However, when the time was elapsed, she came and made her a visit, and very modestly intimated, that now she was up and well, she hoped she should see her abroad again; for that, really, it would be inconvenient for her to be without her kennel any longer, and therefore, she told her, she must be so free as to desire her to provide herself with other lodgings as soon as she could. The lying-in Bitch replied, that truly she was ashamed of having kept her so long out of her own house; but it was not upon her own account (for indeed she was well enough to go any where) so much as that of her puppies, who were yet so weak, that she was afraid they would not be able to follow her; and, if she would be so good as to let her stay a fortnight longer, she would take it as the greatest obligation in the world. The other Bitch was so good-natured and compassionate as to comply with this request also; but at the expiration of the term, came and told her positively that she must turn out, for she could not possibly let her be there a day longer. Must turn out, says the other; we will see to that: for I promise you, unless you can beat me and my whole litter of whelps, you are never likely to have any thing more to do here.

APPLICATION.

WISE and good-natured men do not shut their ears, nor harden their hearts, against the calls of humanity, and the cries of distress; but how often are their generous natures imposed upon by the artifices of the base and worthless! These fail not to lay their plans with deep cunning, to work themselves into the good graces of the benevolent, and having accomplished their ends, the return they often make is abusive language, or the most open acts of violence. One of the evil and lamentable consequences arising out of this, is, that worth in distress suffers by it: for distrust and suspicion take hold of the minds of good men, and the hand of charity is thus benumbed. This Fable may also serve to caution us never to let any thing we value go out of our possession without good security. The man who means to act prudently, ought never to put himself in the power of others, or to run any risk of involving his own family in ruin.

THE HEN AND THE FOX.

A Fox having crept into an out-house, looked up and down, seeking what he might devour, and at last spied a Hen perched up so high, that he could by no means come at her. My dear friend, says he, how do you do? I heard that you were ill, and kept within; at which I was so concerned, that I could not rest till I came to see you. Pray how is it with you now? Let me feel your pulse a little : indeed you do not look well at all. He was running on after this fulsome manner, when the Hen answered him from the roost, Truly, friend Reynard, you are judging rightly, for I never was in more pain in my life : I must beg your pardon for being so free as to tell you that I see no company; and you must excuse me too for not coming down to you, for, to say the truth, my condition is such, that I fear I should catch my death by it.

APPLICATION.

It is generally the design of hypocritical persons to delude and impose upon others, with an eye to derive some benefit to themselves, when they pretend to feel a flattering anxiety for their welfare; or sometimes they may perhaps, with impertinent folly, mean no more than merely to mock and befool men who are weak enough to become their dupes. In both cases they are enemies to truth and sincerity, which adorn and tend so greatly to promote the happiness of society, and they ought to be exposed as such. For although men of penetration see through the pretence, and escape its dangers, yet the weak, the vain, and the unsuspicious are put off their guard, and have not discernment enough to shun the trap so pleasingly baited. The Fable also furnishes a hint against hypocritical legacy hunters, whose regard is generally of the same nature as that of the Fox for the Hen.

THE ASS IN THE LION'S SKIN.

An Ass, while feeding upon the coarse herbage by
the edge of a wood, found a Lion's skin, and putting
it on, went in this disguise into the adjoining forests
and pastures, and threw all the flocks and herds into
the greatest consternation and dismay. At length, his
master, who was in search of him, made his appearance, and the silly beast, entertaining the idea of
frightening him also, capered forward with a terrific
gait towards him; but the good man seeing his long
ears stick out, presently knew him, and with a stout
cudgel made him sensible, that notwithstanding his being dressed in a Lion's skin, he was really no more
than an Ass.

APPLICATION.

As all affectation is wrong, and tends to expose and make a man ridiculous, so the more distant he is from the thing which he affects to appear, the stronger will be the ridicule which he excites, and the greater the inconvenience into which he thereby runs himself. How strangely absurd it is for a timorous person to procure a military post, in order to keep himself out of danger! and to fancy a red coat the surest protection for cowardice! Yet there have been those who have purchased a commission to avoid being insulted; and have been so silly as to think courage was interwoven with a sash, or tied up in a cockade. But it would not be amiss for such gentlemen to consider that it is not in the power of scarlet cloth to alter nature, and that as it is expected a soldier should shew himself a man of courage and intrepidity upon all proper occasions, they may by this means meet the disgrace they intended to avoid, and appear greater Asses than they needed to have done. However, it is not in point of fortitude only that people are liable to expose themselves, by assuming a character to which they are not equal; but he who puts on a shew of learning, of religion, of a superior capacity in any respect, or in short, of any virtue or knowledge, to which he has no proper claim, is, and will always be found to be, an Ass in a Lion's skin.

THE CLOWN AND THE GNAT.

As a clownish Fellow was sitting musing upon a bank, a Gnat alighted upon his leg and bit it. He slapped his hand upon the place, with the intention of of crushing the assailant; but the little nimble insect escaped between his fingers, and repeated its attacks. Every time he struck at it, he gave himself a smart blow upon the leg, but missed his aim. At this he became enraged, and in the height of his peevish and impatient humour, he earnestly prayed to Hercules, beseeching him with his mighty power to stretch forth his arm against a pernicious insect, by which he was so miserably tormented.

APPLICATION.

He who suffers his mind to be ruffled by every little

inconvenience, subjects himself to perpetual uneasiness
and disquiet. There is no accident, however trivial,
but is capable of disconcerting him, and he becomes
absurdly miserable on the most foolish occasion. His
good humour is soured in an instant, and he is rendered uncomfortable to himself, and odious or ridiculous
to all about him. He prays with earnestness to the
Supreme Being to aid him in all his paltry selfish
schemes, or to gratify vanities, for which, as a rational being, he ought to blush and be ashamed. The
imaginary distresses, which his unfortunate disposition
heightens into severe calamities, are matter of diver-
sion to those who are disposed to sneer at him; and
when his pettish humour makes him rave like a mad-
man, and curse his fate, at the dropping of a hat, or
the blunder of a servant, even his friends must view
his behaviour with a mixed emotion of pity and contempt.

THE WOLF AND THE LAMB.

ONE hot sultry day, a Wolf and a Lamb happened to come just at the same time, to quench their thirst in the stream of a brook that fell tumbling down the side of a rocky mountain. The Wolf stood upon the higher ground, and the Lamb at some distance below him. However, the Wolf, having a mind to pick a quarrel with the Lamb, asked him what he meant by disturbing the water, and making it so muddy that he could not drink? and, at the same time, demanded satisfaction. The Lamb, frightened at this threatening charge, told him, in a tone as mild as possible, that with humble submission, he could not conceive how that could be, since the water which he drank ran down from the Wolf to him, and therefore could not be disturbed so far up the stream. Be that as it may, replies the Wolf, you are a rascal, and I have

been told that you used ill language concerning me behind my back, about half a year ago. Upon my word,
says the Lamb, the time you mention was before I was
born. The Wolf, finding it to no purpose to argue
any longer against truth, fell into a great passion,
snarling and foaming at the mouth as if he had been
mad; and drawing nearer to the Lamb, Sirrah, says
he, if it were not you, it was your father, and that is
the same. So he seized the poor innocent helpless
thing, tore it to pieces, and made a meal of it.

APPLICATION.

Where'er oppression rules, fell Wolves devour;
And the worst crimes are want of strength and pow'r.

THEY who do not feel the sentiments of humanity,
will seldom listen to the voice of reason; and when
cruelty and injustice are armed with power, and determined on oppression, the strongest pleas of innocence are preferred in vain, and nothing is more easy
than finding pretences to criminate the unsuspecting
victims of tyranny. How many of the degenerate, corrupt, and arbitrary governments with which the civilized world has been disfigured, have exercised their
vengeance upon the honest and virtuous, who have
dared in bad times to speak the truth; and how many
men in private life are to be met with, whose wolfish
dispositions, and envious and rapacious tempers cannot
bear to see honest industry rear its head !

THE MICE IN COUNCIL.

The Mice called a general council, and after the doors were locked, entered into a free consultation about ways and means how to render themselves more secure from the danger of the Cat. Many schemes were proposed, and much debate took place upon the matter. At last, a young Mouse, in a fine florid speech, broached an expedient, which he contended was the only one to put them entirely out of the power of the enemy, and this was, that the Cat should wear a bell about her neck, which, upon the least motion, would give the alarm, and be a signal for them to retire into their holes. This speech was received with great applause, and it was even proposed by some, that the Mouse who had made it should have the thanks of the assembly. Upon which, an old Mouse, who had sat silent hitherto, gravely observed, that the contrivance was admirable, and the author of it, without doubt, very ingenious; but he thought it would not be so proper to vote him thanks, till he should further inform them how the bell was to be fastened about the Cat's neck, and who would undertake the task.

APPLICATION.

It is easy for visionary projectors to devise schemes, and to descant on their utility, which, after all, are found to be so impracticable, or so difficult, that no man of solid judgment can be prevailed upon to attempt putting them into execution. In all matters where the good of the community is at stake, new projects should be carefully examined in all their bearings, that the ruinous consequences which might follow them may be avoided. All business of this import ought to be left to the decision of such men only as are distinguished for their good sense, probity, honour, and patriotism. When these have examined them in all their different bearings, we may place confidence in their labours, and adopt their plans; but the Fable teaches us not to listen to those rash and ignorant politicians, who are always foisting their schemes upon the public upon every occurrence of mal-administration, without looking beneath the surface, or considering whether they be practicable or otherwise.

THE APE CHOSEN KING.

On the death of the old Lion, without his leaving an heir, the beasts assembled to choose another king of the forest in his stead. The crown was tried on many a head, but did not sit easy upon any one. At length the Ape putting it upon his own, declared that it fitted him quite well, and after shewing them many antic tricks, he with a great deal of grimace, and an affected air of wisdom, offered himself to fill the high office. The silly creatures being pleased with him at the moment, instantly, by a great majority, proclaim- ed him king. The Fox, quite vexed to see his fellow- subjects act so foolishly, resolved to convince them of their sorry choice, and knowing of a trap ready baited, at no great distance, he addressed himself to King Ape, and told him that he had discovered a treasure,

2 c 2

which being found on the waste, belonged to his Majesty. The Ape presently went to take possession of the prize; but no sooner had he laid his paws upon the bait, than he was caught fast in the trap. In this situation, between shame and anger, he chattered out many bitter reproaches against the Fox, calling him rebel and traitor, and threatening revenge: to all which Reynard gravely replied, that this was nothing but a beginning of what he would meet with in the high station his vanity had prompted him to aspire to, as it was only one of the many traps that would be laid for him, and in which he would be caught; but he hoped, this one might be a treasure to him, if it operated as a caution, and served to put him in mind of the false estimate he had put upon his abilities, in supposing, that with his inexperienced empty pate, he could manage the weighty affairs of state. He then, with a laugh, left him to be relieved from his peril by one or other of his foolish loving subjects.

APPLICATION.

WHEN Apes are in power, Foxes will never be wanting to play upon them. Men shew their folly, rashness, and want of consideration, when they elect rulers without the qualifications of integrity and abilities to recommend them to the office; and the higher it is, the more important it is to the interests of the community that it should be properly filled. The Fable also shews the weakness of those who, through self-conceit, aspire to any high station without the requisites to befit them for it, and the want of which exposes authority to scorn.

THE OLD MAN AND DEATH.

A poor feeble old Man, who had crawled from his cottage into a neighbouring wood to gather a few sticks, had made up his bundle, and laying it over his shoulders, was trudging homewards; but what with age, and the length of the way, he grew so faint and weak, that he sunk under it, and as he sat upon the ground, called upon Death to come once for all and ease him of his troubles. Death no sooner heard him, than he came and demanded what he wanted? The poor old Creature, who little thought Death was so near, frightened almost out of his senses with his terrible aspect, answered him trembling, That having by chance let his bundle of sticks fall, and being too infirm to get it up himself, he had made bold to call upon him to help him; and he hoped his worship was not offended with him for the liberty he had taken in craving his assistance.

APPLICATION.

THIS Fable gives us a lively representation of the general behaviour of mankind towards that grim king of terrors, Death. Such liberties do they take with him behind his back, that upon every little accident which happens in their way, Death is immediately called upon, and they even wish it might be lawful for them to finish with their own hands a life so odious, so perpetually tormenting, and vexatious. When, let but Death make his appearance, and the very sense of his near approach almost does the business: then it is that they change their minds, and would be glad to come off so well as to have their old burthen laid upon their shoulders again. But wise and good men know that care and numberless disappointments must be their portion in their passage through life, and know also that it is their duty to endure them with patience; for he is the best and happiest man who neither wishes nor fears the approach of Death.

THE TWO FROGS.

ONE hot sultry summer, the lakes and ponds being almost every where dried up, a couple of Frogs agreed to travel together in search of water. At last they came to a deep well, and sitting upon the brink of it, began to consult whether they should leap in or not. One of them was for it, urging that there was plenty of clear spring water, and no danger of being disturbed. Well, says the other, all this may be true, and yet I cannot come into your opinion for my life; for if the water should happen to dry there too, how should we get out again?

APPLICATION.

In human affairs, many stations we meet,
Where 'tis easy to enter, but hard to retreat.

WE ought never to change our situation in life, nor
undertake any action of importance, without first duly
and deliberately weighing the consequences that may
follow, in all their different bearings. It is commonly
owing to the neglect of such wholesome precautions,
that numbers of young people are led into unfortunate
matches, suddenly made up; and others are from the
same causes led into a round of profuse living, or into
gaming and other extravagant conduct, which is sure to
terminate in ruin. To look before we leap, is a maxim
worthy of being remembered by all ranks and conditions of men, from the lowest to the highest: even
kings may reap benefit by it; for when they inconsi-
derately execute those schemes which their wicked
counsellors advise, they have often abundant reason to
repent. By this blind stupidity, wars are commenced,
from which a state cannot be extricated either with
honour or safety; and unwise projects are encouraged
by the rash accession of those who never considered
the consequences, or how they were to get out, till
they had plunged themselves irrecoverably into them.

THE FOX AND THE BRIAR.

A Fox scrambling hastily over a hedge, in his flight from the hounds, got his foot severely torn by a Briar. Smarting with the pain, he burst into revilings and complaints at this treatment, which he declared he little expected to meet with for only passing over a hedge; and he could not help thinking it was very bad usage to be thus grappled by the long arms, and cut and wounded by the sharp crooked spines of a Briar. True, says the Briar, but recollect that you intended to have made me serve your turn, and would, without ceremony, have trampled me down to the ground: but none of your freedoms with me, Master Reynard; you may make a convenience of others perhaps, but the family of the Briars are not of that cast. Whoever presumes to use any impudent familiarities with them, is sure to smart for it.

2 D

APPLICATION.

PRESUMING and arrogant people do not hesitate to make a convenience, or a kind of stepping stone, of any one who will suffer them to do so ; and if they can only get their turn served, no matter how, they use no cere- mony, nor shew any delicacy in accomplishing their ends.   But the selfish and impudent gentry, who are so apt to take liberties of this kind, now and then mis- take their men, and are justly retorted upon ; and however upon these occasions they may be surprized and angry, others, who are indifferent spectators, in- stead of viewing them as objects of pity, feel a secret satisfaction in seeing them suffer, as proper examples of justice.

THE MAN AND THE WEASEL.

A Man having caught a Weasel in his pantry, was just going to kill it, when the little captive begged that he would not do so cruel a deed, but spare his life; and he assured the Man that he was his friend, and only entered his pantry with a view of destroying the mice with which it was infested. That may be, said the Man, but you do not do this with the intention of serving me, nor with any other view but that of serving yourself; and besides, you are so ferocious and cruel a little creature, that you kill every animal you have within your power, without the least compunction, and seem to delight in killing for killing's sake; therefore, your pretensions to serve me, and your plea for mercy, are good for nothing.

2 D 2

APPLICATION.

MANY people in the world are ever ready to set up the pretensions of their acting with zeal, purely to serve the public, and pretend that it is through the warmth of their friendship that they do the same to individuals; but the main spring of all the actions of the agents of treachery, and of bad men, is set a-going with the view only of serving themselves. It is thus that the unprincipled and mercenary thief-taker would like well to be accounted a public spirited man; and he cannot help boasting of his services as such. The hangman's pretensions are of the same kind: but however useful and necessary some of such a description of men may be, to keep down the wicked part of mankind, who are a nuisance to civilized society, yet the instruments themselves are very like in character to the Weasel in the Fable. The same may be said of those factious writers, who pester the public with their clamorous charges, under the mask of patriotism, but whose real motive is either to gain money by the sale of their highly seasoned scandals, or to run down their corrupt opponents in order to obtain their places.

THE BOAR AND THE ASS.

An Ass happening to meet with a Boar, and being in a frolicsome humour, and having a mind to shew some of his silly wit, began in a sneering familiar style to accost the Boar with, So ho, brother, your humble servant, how is all at home with you? The Boar, nettled at his familiarity, muttered out, Brother indeed! then bristled up towards him, told him he was surprized at his impudence, and was just going to shew his resentment by giving him a rip in the flank: but wisely stifling his passion, he contented himself with only saying, Go, thou sorry beast! I could be easily and amply revenged upon thee; but I dont care to foul my tusks with the blood of so base a creature!

APPLICATION.

It is no uncommon thing to meet with impudent
fools, so very eager of being thought wits, that they
will run great hazards in attempting to shew themselves such, and will often persist in their awkward
raillery to the last degree of offence. But these kind
of folks, instead of raising themselves into esteem, are
held in contempt by men of sense; and though the
generous and the brave may scorn to suffer themselves to be ruffled by the insolent behaviour of every
ass that offends them, yet such sparks must not from
thence conclude, that they will not meet with retorts
in kind from men far superior to themselves in mental
endowments; or that their unseasoned wit will always
escape a more proper, but a different chastisement.

THE DOG AND THE SHEEP.

THE Dog sued the Sheep for a debt, of which the Kite and the Wolf were to be the judges. They, without debating long upon the matter, or making any scruple for want of evidence, gave sentence for the plaintiff, who immediately tore the poor Sheep in pieces, and divided the spoil with the unjust judges.

APPLICATION.

OF the many evils which throw back the well-being of society, none raise in the honest mind more painful and indignant feelings, than beholding the judgment seat of mercy and justice filled by an unjust, corrupt, and wicked judge, who has become, step by step, hardened in his impious enormities, and is the fully-prepared tool and supporter of tyranny and arbitrary power.   Fraud and oppression follow in his train: the righteous laws of a just government are frittered away, or superseded: truth and innocence are obnoxious; honesty is sneered at, and it becomes criminal to espouse the cause of virtue.   In this state of things, wickedness predominates, and its rapacious abettors give full scope to the exercise of all kind of oppression and injustice, to gratify their own vicious lusts.   Then it is that mankind are made to feel the evils of power being in the hands of the worst of their species, who, without hesitation, rob them of their property, and divide the spoils.   If there be not a sufficiency of the most spirited and virtuous patriotism to rescue the country from their fangs, then is despotism and degradation near at hand.

JUPITER AND THE HERDSMAN.

A Herdsman missing a young heifer, went up and down the forest to seek it; and having walked over a great deal of ground to no purpose, he fell a praying to Jupiter for relief, promising to sacrifice a kid to him, if he would help him to a discovery of the thief. After this he went on a little farther, and came near a grove of oaks, where he espied the carcase of his heifer, and a Lion growling over it, and feeding upon it. This sight almost scared him out of his wits; so down he fell upon his knees once more, and addressing himself to Jupiter, O Jupiter, says he, I promised thee a kid to shew me the thief; but now I promise thee a bull, if thou wilt be so merciful as to deliver me out of his clutches.

2 E

APPLICATION.

We ought never to supplicate the Divine power, but through motives of religion and virtue. Prayers dictated by blind self-interest, or to gratify some misguided passion, cannot, it is presumed, be acceptable to the Deity; and of all the involuntary sins which men commit, scarcely any are more frequent than their praying absurdly and improperly, as well as unseasonably, when their time might have been employed to a better purpose. Would men, as they ought to do, obey the commands of Omnipotence, by fulfilling their moral duties, and endeavour with all their might to live as justly as they can, a just Providence would give them what they ought to have: but stupidity and ignorance, until better informed, and divested of superstition and bigotry, will continue to form their notions of the Supreme Being from their own poor shallow conceptions; and nothing contributes more to keep up this injudicious practice among simple, but perhaps well-meaning people, than the numerous collections of those crude rhapsodies, the offspring of itinerant bigotry, with which the country overflows; while most of those prayers are neglected which have been composed with due reflection and matured deliberation, by the most learned and pious of men. This Fable also teaches us, that frequently the gratification of our vain prayers would only lead us into dangers and evils, of the existence of which we had no previous suspicion.

THE OLD LION.

A Lion, that in the prime of his life had been very rapacious and cruel, was reduced by age and infirmities to extreme feebleness. Several of the beasts of the forest, who had been great sufferers by him, now came and revenged themselves upon him. The Boar ripped him with his tusks, the Bull gored him with his horns, and others in various ways had each a stroke at him. When the Ass saw that they might do all this without any danger, he also came and threw his heels in the Lion's face. Upon which, the poor expiring tyrant is said to have groaned out these words: Alas! how grievous is it to suffer insults, even from the brave and valiant; but to be spurned at by so base a creature as this, is worse than dying ten thousand deaths!

APPLICATION.

When men in power lose sight of justice and mercy, and cruelly and unjustly tyrannise over the people under their sway, they never will gain sincere reverence or respect from the rest of mankind. The injuries they inflict in the hey-day of their wicked career, will be remembered with detestation through life; and when age and impotence lay hold of them, they must not expect to meet with friends they never deserved; but may be certain of being treated with neglect and contempt, and the baser their enemies are, the more insolent and intolerable will be the affront. It will then be discovered, with bitter remorse, that the days have passed away, in which virtue and dignity ought to have laid the foundation of a reputation which would have been the solace of old age, and also extended a good name to posterity with feelings of veneration; instead of which the remembrance of past crimes will haunt the guilty mind, and the unjust man will at last be thrown into the grave with the common dust, amidst the whispers of " Let him go," and he will be no more remembered than the animals on which he feasted, or the herbage which was cut down when he was a child.

THE MAGPIE AND THE SHEEP.

A Magpie sat chattering upon the back of a Sheep, and pulling off the wool to line her nest. Peace, you noisy thing, says the Sheep: if I were a dog, you durst not serve me so. That is true enough, replies the Magpie, I know very well whom I have to deal with: I never meddle with the surly and revengeful; but I love to plague such poor helpless creatures as you are, who cannot do me any harm.

APPLICATION.

IT is the characteristic of a mean, low, base spirit, to be insolent or tyrannical to those who are obliged to submit to it, and slavishly submissive to those who have the spirit and the power to resist. Men of this stamp take especial care not to meddle with people of their own malicious principles, for fear of meeting with a suitable return; but they delight in doing mischief for mischief's sake, and seem pleased when they can insult the innocent with impunity. This kind of behaviour is inconsistent with all the rules of honour and generosity, and is opposite to every thing that is great, good, amiable, and praise-worthy.

THE FOX AND THE STORK.

THE Fox invited the Stork to dinner, and, being disposed to divert himself at the expence of his guest, provided nothing for the entertainment but soup, which he served up in a wide shallow dish. This the Fox could lap up with a great deal of ease; but the Stork, who could but just dip in the point of his bill, was not a bit the better for his entertainment. However, a few days after, he returned the compliment, and invited the Fox; but suffered nothing to be brought to table excepting some minced meat in a glass jar, the neck of which was so deep, and so narrow, that, though the Stork with his long bill made a shift to fill his belly, all that the Fox, who was very hungry, could do, was to lick the brims as the Stork slabbered them with his eating. Reynard was heartily vexed at

first; but when he came to take his leave, owned in-
genuously, that he had been used as he deserved; and
that he had no reason to take any treatment ill, of
which himself had set the example.

APPLICATION.

It is very imprudent, as well as uncivil, to affront
any one, and we should always reflect, before we rally
another, whether we can bear to have the jest retorted.
Whoever takes the liberty to exercise his witty talent
in that way, must not be surprised if he meet reprisals
in the end. Indeed, if all those who are thus paid in
their own coin, would take it with the same frankness
that the Fox did, the matter would not be much; but
we are too apt, when the jest comes to be turned home
upon ourselves, to think that insufferable in another
which we looked upon as pretty and facetious when
the humour was our own. The rule of doing as we
would be done by, so proper to be our model in every
transaction of life, may more particularly be of use in
this respect. People seldom or never receive any advantage by these little ludicrous impositions; and yet,
if they were to ask themselves the question, would find,
that they would receive the same treatment from another with a very bad grace.

THE COUNTRYMAN AND THE SNAKE.

A Villager found a Snake under a hedge, almost
dead with cold. Having compassion on the poor creature, he brought it home, and laid it upon the hearth
near the fire, where it had not lain long before it re-
vived with the heat, and began to erect itself, and fly
at the wife and children of its preserver, filling the
whole cottage with its frightful hissings. The Countryman hearing an outcry, came in, and perceiving
how the matter stood, took up a mattock, and soon
dispatched the ingrate, upbraiding him at the same
time in these words: Is this, vile wretch, the reward
you make to him that saved your life? Die, as you
deserve; but a single death is too good for you.

APPLICATION.

THERE are some minds so depraved, and entirely abandoned to wickedness, so dead to all virtuous feelings, that the tenderness and humanity of others, though exerted in their own favour, not only fail to make a proper impression of gratitude upon them, but are not able to restrain them from repaying benevolence with injuries. Moralists, in all ages, have incessantly declaimed against the enormity of this crime, concluding that they who are capable of injuring their benefactors, are not fit to live in a community; being such as the natural ties of parent, friend, or country are too weak to restrain within the bounds of society. Indeed, the sin of ingratitude is so detestable, that none but the basest tempers can be guilty of it. Men of low grovelling minds, who have been rescued from indigence by the hand of benevolence, or of charity, forget their benefactors, as well as their original wretchedness; and as soon as prosperity flows upon them, it too often serves only to rekindle their native rancour and venom, and they hiss and brandish their tongues against those who are so inadvertent or unfortunate as to have served them. But prudent people need not to be admonished on this subject; for they know how much it behoves them to beware of taking a snake into their bosom.

THE COCK AND THE FOX.

A Cock, perched upon a lofty tree, crowed so loud, that his voice echoed through the wood, and drew to the place a Fox, who was prowling in quest of prey. But Reynard finding the Cock was inaccessible, had recourse to stratagem to decoy him down. Approaching the tree, Cousin, says he, I am heartily glad to see you; but I cannot forbear expressing my uneasiness at the inconvenience of the place, which will not let me pay my respects to you in a better manner, though I suppose you will come down presently, and that difficulty will be removed. Indeed, cousin, says the Cock, to tell you the truth, I do not think it safe to venture upon the ground; for, though I am convinced how much you are my friend, yet I may have the misfortune to fall into the clutches of some other beast,

and what will become of me then? O dear, says Reynard, is it possible you do not know of the peace that
has been so lately proclaimed between all kinds of birds
and beasts; and that we are for the future to forbear
hostilities, and to live in harmony, under the severest
penalties. All this while the Cock seemed to give little
attention to what was said, but stretched out his neck
as if he saw something at a distance. Cousin, says the
Fox, what is that you look at so earnestly? Why,
says the Cock, I think I see a pack of hounds yonder,
a good way off. O then, says the Fox, your humble
servant, I must be gone. Nay, pray cousin do not go,
says the Cock, I am just coming down; sure you are
not afraid of the dogs in these peaceable times. No,
no, says he; but ten to one whether they have yet
heard of the proclamation!

APPLICATION.

THE moral of this Fable principally instructs us not
to be too credulous in believing the insinuations of
those who are already distinguished by their want of
faith and honesty, for perfidious people ought ever to
be suspected in the reports that favour their own interest. When, therefore, any such would draw us
into a compliance with their destructive measures, by
a pretended civility, or plausible relation, we should
consider such proposals as a bait, artfully placed to
conceal some fatal hook, which is intended to draw us
into danger; and if by any simple counterplot we can
unmask the design and defeat the schemes of the wicked, it will not only be innocent, but praise-worthy.

THE HARE AND THE TORTOISE.

A Hare vainly boasting of her great speed in running, and casting a look of disdain upon a Tortoise, that was slowly moving along, What a poor crawling thing are you! said she: I can go over a territory of country with the velocity of the wind, while you are an hour in accomplishing a journey of half a furlong. In a race I could leave you twenty miles behind me, in the time you were about reaching the end of one. I don't know that, said the Tortoise, and will give you a trial. Upon this, a match was made to run a certain distance, and the Fox, who had heard the dispute, was chosen umpire of the race. They then started together, and away went the Hare with great swiftness, and soon left the Tortoise out of sight, and thinking herself certain of winning the race, she made a jest of the matter, squatted down in a tuft of fern,

and took a nap, concluding she could easily make up
the lost ground, should the Tortoise at any time pass
by.   Indulging in this security, she over-slept herself,
until the Tortose, in a continued steady pace, arrived
first at the fixed distance, and won the race.

APPLICATION.

WE must not flatter ourselves with coming to the
end of our journey in time, if we sleep by the way;
and unnecessary delays, in all pressing affairs, are just
so much time lost.   Action is an important part of the
business of life; and " up and be doing" is a motto we
ought to keep in mind, as it has guided many a plain
plodding man, with steady aim, to carry his point effectually in making his own fortune, and at the same
time gaining the esteem of the world.   Industry and
application to business make amends for the want of a
quick and ready wit; but men of great natural abilities, and vivacity of imagination, often presume too
much upon the superiority of their genius, and if to
this presumption they add pride and conceit, they despise the drudgery of business, and suffer their affairs
to go to disorder or ruin, through idleness and neglect.

THE BLACKAMOOR.

A Man having bought a Blackamoor, was so simple as to think that the colour of his skin was only dirt which he had contracted for want of due care under his former master. This fault he fancied might easily be removed by washing, so he ordered the poor Black to be put into a tub, and was at a considerable charge in providing ashes, soap, and scrubbing brushes for the operation. To work they went, rubbing and scouring his skin all over, but to no manner of purpose: for when they had repeated their washings several times, and were grown quite weary, all they got by it was, that the Blackamoor caught cold and died.

APPLICATION.

" What's bred in the bone will never come out of
the flesh."

NATURE cannot by any art or labour be changed;
she may indeed be wrought upon and moulded by
good council and discipline; but it is in vain to attempt a total transformation of our genius, person, or
complexion: therefore our application, assiduity, and
pains, when wrong directed, are of no avail. We
should, indeed, strive to discover which way the bent
of our genius lies, that we may apply ourselves to a
judicious cultivation and improvement of it; but we
ought to be sure never to thwart or oppose nature's
fixed laws. When men aspire to eminence in any of
the various arts or sciences, without being gifted with
the innate powers or abilities for such attainments, it
is only like attempting to wash the Blackamoor white.

THE LION IN LOVE.

THE Lion by chance saw a fair maid, the forester's daughter, as she was tripping over a lawn, and fell in love with her. Nay, so violent was his passion, that he could not live unless he made her his own; therefore, without more delay, he broke his mind to the father, and demanded the damsel for his wife. The man, odd as the proposal seemed at first, soon recollected that, by complying, he might get the Lion into his power; but, by refusing him, should only exasperate and provoke his rage. Accordingly, he seemed to consent; but told him it must be upon these conditions: that, considering the girl was young and tender, he must let his teeth be plucked out, and his claws be cut off, lest he should hurt her, or at least frighten her with the apprehension of them. The Lion was too much in love to hesitate; but was no sooner deprived

2 G

of his teeth and claws, than the treacherous forester attacked him with a huge club, and knocked out his brains.

Of all the ill consequences that may attend the blind passion of love, few prove so fatal as that of its drawing people into a sudden and ill-concerted marriage. In the midst of a fit of madness, they commit a rash act, of which, as soon as they come to themselves, they find reason to repent as long as they live. Many an unthinking young man has been treated as much like a savage in this respect as the Lion in the Fable. He has, perhaps, had nothing valuable belonging to him but his estate, and the documents which formed his title to it; and if he is so far captivated, as to be persuaded to part with these, his teeth and his claws are gone, and he lies entirely at the mercy of madam and her relations, who will most likely not fail to keep him in complete subjection, after they have stripped him of all his power. Nothing but a true friendship, and a mutual interest, can keep up a reciprocal love between the conjugal pair, and when these are wanting, contempt and aversion soon step in to supply their place. Matrimony then becomes a state of downright enmity and hostility; and what a miserable case he must be in, who has put himself and his whole power into the hands of his enemy. Let those reflect upon this (while they are in their sober senses) who abhor the thoughts of being betrayed into their ruin, by following the impulse of a blind unheeding passion.

THE FOX AND THE HEDGEHOG.

A Fox, in swimming across a river, was forced down by the rapidity of the stream to a place where the bank was so steep and slippery, that he could not ascend it. While he was struggling in this situation, a swarm of flies settled on his head and eyes, and tormented him grievously. A Hedgehog, who saw and pitied his condition, offered to call in the assistance of the Swallow to drive them away. No, no, friend, replies the Fox, I thank you for your kind offer; but it is better to let this swarm alone, for they are already pretty well filled, and should they be driven away, a fresh and more hungry set would succeed them, and suck me until I should not have a drop of blood left in my veins.

APPLICATION.

This Fable is recorded by Aristotle, who tells us that Æsop spoke it to the Samians on occasion of a popular sedition, to dissuade them from deposing their great minister of state, lest they might, in getting rid of one who was already glutted with their spoils, make room for a more hungry and rapacious one in his stead. By this it would appear, that some ministers of state in ancient times, instead of being guided by integrity and patriotism, were intent only upon filling their own coffers, and aggrandizing and enriching their own relations, from the plunder of the people whose affairs they were entrusted with; and that they considered them as their prey, rather than their charge. A succession of such ministers, who can be countenanced by weak monarchs only, is more calamitous to a nation than plague, pestilence, and famine; for the effects of their mal-administration do not end with their wicked lives, but lay the foundation of ruin to nations that would, under a patriotic government, have been virtuous, great, and flourishing.

THE SPARROW AND THE HARE.

A Hare being seized by an Eagle, squeaked out in a most woful manner. A Sparrow, that sat upon a tree just by, and saw the affair, could not forbear being unseasonably witty, but called out to the Hare: So, ho! what, sit there and be killed! prithee up and away; I dare say if you would but try, so swift a creature as you are would easily escape from an Eagle. As he was going on with his cruel raillery, down came a Hawk and snapped him up, and notwithstanding his cries and lamentations, fell to devouring him in an instant. The Hare, who was just expiring, addressing her last words to the Sparrow, said, You who just now insulted my misfortune, with so much security as you thought, may please to shew us how well you can bear the like, now it has befallen you.

APPLICATION.

To insult people in distress, is the characteristic of a cruel, indiscreet, and giddy temper; and he must surely have a very bad heart, and no very good head, who can look on the day of grief, and the hour of distress, as a time for impertinent raillery. If any other arguments were necessary, or might be supposed capable of enforcing moral precepts on those who cannot be actuated by humanity, it might be added, that the vicissitudes of human affairs render such behaviour imprudent, as well as barbarous; since we cannot tell how soon we may be ourselves reduced to lament the woes which are now the objects of our derision: for nobody knows whose turn may be the next.

THE MAN AND HIS TWO WIVES.

A Man, in times when polygamy was allowed, had two wives, one of whom, like himself, had seen her best days, and was verging upon the decline of life, but possessed many engaging qualities. The other was young and beautiful, and shared the affection of her husband, whom she made as happy as he was capable of being, but was not completely so herself. The white hairs mixed with the black upon the good man's head, gave her some uneasiness, by proclaiming the great disparity of their years; wherefore, under colour of dressing his head, she plucked out the silver hairs, that he might still have as few visible signs of an advanced age as possible. The older dame, for reasons directly opposite, esteemed these grey locks as the honours of his head, and thought, while they gave him a venerable look, they made her appear something younger, so that every time she combed his head, she took equal pains to extirpate the black hairs. Each continued her project, unknown to the other, until the poor man, who thought their desire to oblige him put them upon this extraordinary officiousness in dressing his head, found himself without any hair at all !

APPLICATION.

As christianity has banished polygamy, no immediate moral can be derived by husbands from this Fable, unless we conclude, that it is as impossible to serve two mistresses as two masters; for whatever we do to please the one, will probably offend the other. To conciliate the affections of persons whose tempers are opposite, is extremely difficult, if not impracticable. To wives it may teach, that those whose love is tempered with a tolerable share of good sense, will be sure to have no separate views of their own, nor do any thing immediately relating to their husbands, without consulting them first. All that we shall add to what has been said, is to observe, that many women may ignorantly, out of a pure effect of complaisance, do a thousand disagreeable things to their husbands. But in a married state, one party should not be guessing at or presuming, but inform themselves certainly, what will please the other; and if a wife use her husband like a friend only, the least she can do is first to communicate to him all the important enterprizes she undertakes, and especially those which she intends should be for his honour and advantage.

MERCURY AND THE CARVER.

MERCURY being very desirous to know what credit he had obtained in the world, and how he was esteemed among mankind, disguised himself, and went to the shop of a famous Statuary, where images were to be sold. He saw Jupiter, Juno, and himself, and most of the other gods and goddesses: so, pretending that he wanted to buy, he asked the prices of several, and at length pointing to Jupiter, What, says he, is the lowest price you will take for that? A crown, says the other; and what for that? pointing to Juno: I must have something more for that. Mercury then, casting his eye upon the figure of himself, with all his symbols about it, Here am I, said he to himself, in quality of Jupiter's messenger, and the patron of artisans, with all my trades about me; and then smiling with a self-sufficient air, and pointing to the image, and pray

2 H

friend, what is the price of this elegant figure? Oh, replied the Statuary, if you will buy Jupiter and Juno, I will throw you that into the bargain.

APPLICATION.

If we knew ourselves, of what could any of us be vain? Vanity is the fruit of ignorance, and the froth of perverted pride. Humility is the constant attendant on men of great talents and good qualities: these enable them to see how far they are short of perfection; but the vain and arrogant conceive they have attained its height. All vain men, who affect popularity, fancy other people have the same opinion of them that they have of themselves; but nothing makes them look so cheap and little in the eyes of discerning people as their enquiring (like Mercury in the Fable) after their own worth, and wanting to know what value others set upon them: and those who are so full of themselves, as to hunt for praise, and lay traps for commendation, will generally be disappointed, and be marked out as the emptiest of fellows; for it argues a littleness of mind to be too anxious and solicitous concerning our fame. He that behaves himself as he should do, need not fear procuring a good share of respect, and a fair reputation; but then these should not be the end or the motive of our pursuits: our principal aim should be the welfare of our country, our friends, and ourselves, and should be directed by the rules of honour and virtue.

THE FOX AND THE GOAT.

A Fox having tumbled, by chance, into a well, had been ineffectually endeavouring a long while to get out again, when, at last, a Goat came to the place, and wanting to drink, asked Reynard whether the water was good? Good! said he, aye, so sweet, that I am afraid I have surfeited myself, I have drank so abundantly. The Goat, upon this, without more consideration, leapt in; when the Fox mounted upon his back, and taking the advantage of his horns, bounded up in an instant, and left the poor simple Goat at the bottom of the well to shift for himself. Upon the Goat's reproaching him for his perfidy, Ah, Master Goat, said he, you have far more hairs in your beard than brains in your head.

APPLICATION.

CREDULITY may be said to be the child of ignorance, and the mother of distress. A wise man will not suffer himself to be imposed upon by slender artifices and idle tales; but the credulous man is easily deluded, and subjects himself to numberless misfortunes. He is ever the dupe of designing knaves, and of needy adventurers, who are always intent upon serving themselves at the expence of others. They fasten upon opulent men of weak minds, as the objects of delusion, and for this purpose, tempt them with proposals of apparently advantageous schemes, which they have ready made out, to entice their victims to embark along with them. By credulity, they hope to establish their own fortune, and provided this be done, they care not, even if the ruin of their unsuspecting associates follow. It will likewise ever be found that when an honest man and a knave happen to become partners in the same common interest, the latter, whenever necessity pinches, will be sure to shift for himself, and leave the former in the lurch.

JUNO AND THE PEACOCK.

THE Peacock complained to Juno, how hardly he was used in not having so good a voice as the Nightingale. That little bird, says he, charms every ear with his melody, while my hoarse screamings disgust every one who hears them. The Goddess, concerned at the uneasiness of her favourite bird, answered him very kindly to this purpose: If the Nightingale be blest with a fine voice, you have the advantage in point of beauty and majesty of person. Ah! said the Peacock, but what avails my silent unmeaning beauty, when I am so far excelled in voice? The Goddess dismissed him with this advice: Consider that the properties of every creature were appointed by the decree of fate: to you beauty; strength to the Eagle; to the Nightingale a voice of melody; the faculty of speech to the Parrot;

and to the Dove innocence.   Each of these is contented with his own peculiar quality; and unless you have
a mind to be miserable, you must learn to be so too.

APPLICATION.

THE most useful lesson that we can possibly learn,
towards the attainment of happiness in this world, is
to enjoy those blessings that we have in our power,
without vainly pining after those which we have not.
Instead of being ambitious of having more endowments
than nature has allotted to us, we should spare no
pains to cultivate those we have; and which a sourness or peevishness of temper, instead of improving,
will certainly lessen and impair.   Whoever neglects
the happiness within his reach, in order to brood over
the consideration of how much happier he might have
been, had his situation been like that of others, inge-
niously contrives to torment himself, and opens a perpetual source of discontent, which prevents his ever
being at ease.   He does not reflect, or he would soon
discover, that all the desirable properties in the world
never centered in one man, and that those who have
had the greatest share of them, if of an unhappy disposition, still wished for something more, and wanted to
possess some inherent gifts which shone forth in other
men : but such persons ought to be put in mind, that
it does not become mortals to repine at the will of
Heaven, which distributes happiness with an equal
hand upon the highest and the lowest of mankind, if
they were wise enough, and grateful enough, to perceive it.

THE LION AND OTHER BEASTS.

THE Lion having entered into an alliance with other Beasts of prey, it was agreed, for their mutual advantage, that they should hunt in company, and divide the spoil. They accordingly met on a certain day, and commenced the chase, and ere long they ran down and killed a fine fat Deer, which was instantly divided into four parts, there happening to be then only the Lion and three others present. After the division was made, the Lion advancing forward with an air of majesty, and pointing to one of the shares, was pleased to declare himself after the following manner: This I take possession of as my right, which devolves to me, as I am descended by a true, lineal, hereditary succession from the royal family of Lion: that, pointing to the second, I claim by, I think, no unreasonable title, considering that the success of all the engagements

you have with the enemy depends chiefly upon my
courage and conduct; and you very well know that
wars are too expensive to be carried on without large
supplies. Then, nodding his head towards the third,
that I shall take by virtue of my prerogative, to which
I make no question but so dutiful and loyal a people
will pay all the deference and regard that I can desire.
Now, as for the remaining part, the necessity of our
present affairs is so very urgent, our stock so low, and
our credit so impaired and weakened, that I must insist upon your granting that without hesitation or de-
mur; and hereof fail not at your peril.

APPLICATION.

No alliance is safe which is made with the wicked, if
they be superior to us in power. The most solemn
treaties will be disregarded as soon as they can be broken with advantage. Powerful potentates, when they
are regardless of moral obligation, and consider might
only to be right, will never want specious pretences to
furbish out their declarations of war, nor hesitate about
inveigling less powerful states to join them, and after
subduing the enemy, and seizing upon the spoils, will
fall upon their allies on the slightest pretences, or for
no better reason but because they are powerful enough
to do so. No man ought to be entrusted with unlimited power; and when a community has been stupid
enough to put the management of their affairs into such
hands, they have ever found their confidence abused,
and their property invaded.

JUPITER AND PALLAS.

ONCE upon a time, the Heathen Gods agreed to adopt each a particular tree into their patronage. Jupiter chose the Oak; Venus was pleased to name the Myrtle; Apollo pitched upon the Laurel; Cybele took the Pine; and Hercules the Poplar. Pallas being present, expressed her surprise at their fancy, in making choice of trees that bore nothing. Oh, says Jupiter, the reason of that is plain enough, for we would not be thought to dispense our favours with any mercenary view. You may do as you please, says she, but let the Olive be my tree; and I declare my reason for choosing it is, because it bears plenty of noble useful fruit. Upon which the Thunderer, putting on a serious composed gravity, spoke thus to the Goddess: Indeed daughter, it is not without cause that you are so celebrated for your wisdom; for unless some benefit attend our actions, to perform them for the sake of glory is but a silly business.

APPLICATION.

In all our actions, we should intend something useful and beneficial; for the standing value of all things is in proportion to their use. To undertake affairs with no other view but that of empty glory, whatever some curious dreamers may fancy, is employing our time after a very foolish manner. The Almighty created the world out of his infinite goodness, for the good of his creatures, and not out of a passion for glory, which is a vain, silly, mean principle; and when we talk of glorifying the Author of our being, if we think reasonably, we must mean shewing our gratitude to him, by imitating this goodness of his, as far as we are able, and endeavouring to make some good or other the aim of all our undertakings. For if empty glory be unworthy the pursuit of a wise man, how vastly improper must it be to make an offering of it to an all-wise Deity.

THE VIPER AND THE FILE.

A Viper having entered a smith's shop, looked up and down for something to eat; when, casting his eye upon a file, he greedily seized upon it, and fell to gnawing it with his teeth. After he had spent some time in his attempts to devour it, the File told him very gruffly, that he had better be quiet and let him alone; for he would get very little by nibbling at one who, upon occasion, could bite iron and steel.

APPLICATION.

THIS Fable is levelled at those spiteful people who take so malignant a pleasure in the design of hurting others, as not to feel and understand that they hurt only themselves; and at those who are blinded by envy, which prompts them rather than not bite at all, to fall foul where they cannot expect their nibbling will meet with any thing but disappointment, as every one must who is biting at that which is too hard for his teeth. Thus it is that spite and malignity, which are twin brothers, and the offspring of envy, are, as well as their parent, their own tormentors. They intend that the wounds they inflict should be deadly, and the greatest wits and brightest characters in all ages have been the objects of their attacks; but the brilliancy of truth and justice at length shines forth, and shews the deformity of such characters in the clearest light. Other people, of the same character and disposition, though of minor consideration indeed, ought not to be passed over unnoticed. These may be called nibblers, who let their tongues slip very freely, in censuring the actions of persons who, in the esteem of the world, are of such an unquestionable reputation, that nobody will believe what is insinuated against them, and of such influence through their own veracity, that the least word from them would ruin the credit of such adversaries to all intents and purposes. The efforts of little villains of this stamp, like dirty liquor squirted against the wind, recoil back and bespatter their own faces; or like the shades of a picture, serve to set off the brilliant tints of the opposite virtues, which support and adorn society.

THE WOLF IN SHEEP'S CLOTHING.

A Wolf disguising himself in the skin of a sheep, and getting in among the flock, easily caught and devoured many of them. At last the Shepherd discovered him, and cunningly watched the opportunity of slipping a noose about his neck, and immediately hung him up on the branch of a tree. Some other Shepherds observing what he was about, drew near and expressed their surprize at it. Brother Shepherd! says one of them, what! are you hanging your sheep? No, replies the other, but I am hanging a Wolf in Sheep's clothing, and shall never fail to do the same, whenever I can catch one of them in that garb. The Shepherds then expressed themselves pleased at his dexterity, and applauded the justice of the execution.

APPLICATION.

WE ought not to judge of men by their looks, or their dress and appearances, but by the character of their lives and conversation, and by their works; for when we do not examine these, we must not be surprized if we find that we have mistaken evil for good, and instead of an innocent sheep, taken a wolf in disguise under our protection. The finished hypocrite, by assuming the character of virtue, makes the vice more odious and abominable, and when the mask is torn off, and fraud and imposture are detected, every honest man rejoices in the punishment of the offender. Men who have not had good, religious, and moral principles early instilled into their minds, find no barrier to check their propensity to evil, and get hardened as they advance in years; and even the most liberal education, if it want the foundation of truth and honesty, is often a curse instead of a blessing, and the objects of it fail to do honour either to themselves or to their country. Thus it is we see tyranny stalking along under the mask of care and protection. Injustice sets up the letter of the law against its spirit. Oppression strips the widow and the orphan, and at the same time preaches up mercy and compassion. Treachery covers itself under a cloak of kindness; and above all, it is peculiarly-painful to find numbers of men, even of the learned professions, who ought to set an example of probity and honour, misapply their abilities to twist and pervert the sacred meaning of both law and gospel to the basest and worst of purposes.

THE STAG IN THE OX-STALL.

A Stag, pursued by the hunters, took refuge in a stable, and begged of the Oxen, to suffer him to conceal himself under the straw in one of the stalls. They told him that he would be in great danger there, for both the master and the servants would soon come to fodder them, and then he might be sure of meeting his doom. Ah! says the Stag, if you will be so good as not betray me, I hope I shall be safe enough. Presently, in came a servant, who gave a careless look around, and then went out without any discovery. All the other servants of the farm came and went like the first. Upon this, the Stag began to exult, imagining himself quite secure; but a shrewd old Ox told him that he was reckoning upon his safety too soon, for there was another person to come, by whom he would not so readily be looked over. Accordingly, by and by came the master, who carefully peeped into every corner, and at last, in turning over the litter, discovered the Stag's horns sticking out of the straw : upon which, he called all his servants back, and soon made prize of the poor creature.

APPLICATION.

THIS Fable is levelled against those worthless hirelings, who slide over their time in negligent disorder, and this not so much for want of capacity as honesty; their own private interest almost solely occupying their attention, while that of their master, whose wages they receive, and whose bread they eat, is postponed, or entirely neglected. Such servants deserve not to be inmates in any good man's house; but where they are, it is absolutely necessary for the governors of families to look into their affairs with their own eyes; for though they may happen not to be in personal danger from the treachery of their domestics, they are perpetually liable to injuries from their negligence, which leaves the master open to the artifices of those who would defraud him. Few families are reduced to poverty merely by their own extravagance: the inattention of servants swells every article of expence in domestic economy; and the retinue of great men, instead of exerting their industry to increase their master's wealth, commonly exercise no other office than that of caterpillars, to consume and devour it. The fate of the Stag also warns us not to engage in any hazardous speculation, the success of which is to depend upon the ignorance or carelessness of those with whom we have to deal; for though we may over-reach one or two, yet some master-eye is sure at last to pierce our covering of straw, and make us pay dearly for deviating from the straight road of candour and prudence.

THE FOWLER AND THE RING-DOVE.

A Fowler took his gun, and went into the woods a-shooting. He spied a Ring-dove among the branches of an Oak, and clapping the piece to his shoulder, took his aim, and made himself sure of killing it. But just as he was going to pull the trigger, an Adder, which he had trod upon under the grass, bit him so painfully in the leg, that he was obliged to quit his design, and throw his gun down in an agony. The venom immediately infected his blood, and his whole body began to mortify; which, when he perceived, he could not help owning it to be just. Fate, says he, has brought destruction upon me, while I was contriving the death of another.

2 K

APPLICATION.

THE mischief that bad men meditate to others, commonly, like a judgment, falls upon their own heads;
and the punishment of wickedness is so just in itself,
that the sufferer, who has made others feel it, cannot,
if he think rightly, but confess that he deserves the
like inflicted on himself.   The hardened unfeeling
heart of a cruel and unjust man, can, however, continue to do a thousand bitter things to others, until he
tastes calamity himself, and then only it is that he feels
the insupportable uneasiness it occasions.   Why should
we think others born to hard treatment more than
ourselves, or imagine it can be reasonable to do to
another what we should think very hard to suffer in
our own persons?

THE HARES AND THE FROGS.

THE Hares in a certain park having met to consult
upon some plan to preserve themselves from their numerous enemies, all agreed that life was full of care
and misery, and that they saw no prospect of things
changing for the better.   Full of these desponding
thoughts, and just as it had been proposed that they
should put an end to their existence, a storm arose,
which tore the branches from the trees, and whirled the
leaves about their ears.   Panic-struck, they ran like
mad creatures, until they were stopped by a lake, into
which they hastily resolved to throw themselves headlong, rather than lead a life so full of dangers and
crosses: but upon their approaching its margin, a number of Frogs, which were sitting there, frightened at
their sudden approach, in the greatest confusion leapt
into the water, and dived to the bottom; which an old

2 K 2

Hare, more sedate than the rest, observing, called out,
Have a care what ye do! Here are other creatures I
perceive, which have their fears as well as we. Dont
then let us fancy ourselves the most miserable of any
upon earth; but rather, by their example, learn to
bear patiently those inconveniences which nature has
thrown upon us.

APPLICATION.

This Fable is designed to shew us how unreasonable many people are, who live in continual fears and
disquiet about the miserableness of their condition.
There is hardly any state of life great enough to satisfy the wishes of an ambitious man; and scarcely any
so mean, but may supply the necessities of him that is
moderate. There are few beings so very wretched,
that they cannot pick out others in a more deplorable
situation, and with whom they would not change cases.
The rich man envies the poor man's health, without
considering his wants; and the poor man envies the
other's treasure, without considering his diseases. The
miseries of others should serve to add vigour to our
minds, and teach us to bear up against the load of
lighter misfortunes. But what shall we say to those
who have a way of creating themselves panics from
the rustling of the wind, the scratching of a rat or a
mouse behind the hangings, the fluttering of a moth,
or the motion of their own shadow by moon-light!
Their whole life is as full of alarms as that of a Hare,
and they never think themselves so easy as when, like
the timorous folks in the Fable, they meet with a set
of creatures as fearful as themselves.

THE MOUNTAINS IN LABOUR.

THE Mountains were said to be in labour, and uttered the most dreadful groans. People came together,
far and near, to see what birth would be produced;
and after they had waited a considerable time in expectation, out crept a Mouse.

APPLICATION.

PROJECTORS of all kinds, who endeavour by artful
rumours, large promises, and vast preparations, to
raise the expectations of mankind, and then by their
mean performances disappoint them, have, time out of
mind, been lashed with the recital of this Fable. It
should teach us to suspect those who promise very
largely, and to examine cautiously what grounds they
proceed upon, and whether their pretensions are not

intended to render us their tools, or the dupes of their artifices. It likewise teaches us not to rely implicitly upon those constant declarations for liberty and the public good, which artful politicians use as stepping stones to power; but who having raised the people's expectations to the highest pitch, and obtained their desire by the public enthusiasm, then turn their whole art and-cunning to embezzling the public treasure for their own private wicked ends, or to ruin and enslave their country; or at best but imitate the bad conduct of those whom they turned out by their clamour, while the sanguine hopes of all those that wished well to virtue, and flattered themselves with a reformation of every thing that opposed the well-being of the community, vanish away in smoke, and are lost in a gloomy uncomfortable prospect. The Fable likewise intimates, that the uncertain issue of all human undertakings should induce us not to make pompous boasts of ourselves, but to guard against promising any thing exceedingly great, for fear of coming off with a production ridiculously little. If we set out modestly, and perform more than we engaged to do, we shall find our fame grow upon us, and every unexpected addition we make to our plan will raise us more and more in the good opinion of the world; but if, on the contrary, we make ample professions of the greatness of our designs, and the excellence of our own abilities, it will too often happen, that instead of swelling our reputation, we shall only blow the trumpet to our shame.

THE VAIN JACK-DAW.

A certain Jack-daw was so proud and ambitious, that, not contented to live within his own sphere, he picked up the feathers which fell from the Peacocks, stuck them in among his own, and very confidently introduced himself into an assembly of those beautiful birds. They soon found him out, stripped him of his borrowed plumes, and falling upon him with their sharp bills, punished him as his presumption deserved. Upon this, full of grief and affliction, he returned to his old companions, and would have lived with them again; but they, knowing his late life and conversation, industriously avoided him, and refused to admit him into their company; and one of them, at the same time, gave him this serious reproof: If, friend, you could have been contented with our station, and had not disdained the rank in which nature had placed you, you had not been used so scurvily by those upon whom you intruded yourself, nor suffered the notorious slight which now we think ourselves obliged to put upon you.

APPLICATION.

To aim at making a figure by the means of either borrowed wit, or borrowed money, generally subjects us at last to a ten-fold ridicule. A wise man, therefore, will take his post quietly, in his own station, without pretending to fill that of another, and never affect to look bigger than he really is, by means of a false or borrowed light. It shews great weakness and vanity in any man to be pleased at making an appearance above what he really is; but if to enable him to do so with something of a better grace, he has clandestinely feathered his nest out of his neighbour's goods, it is a pity if he should not be found out, stripped of his plunder, and treated like a felonious rogue into the bargain.

THE LION AND THE MOUSE.

A Lion having laid down to take his repose under the spreading boughs of a shady tree, a company of Mice scampered over his back and waked him. Upon which, starting up, he clapped his paw upon one of them, and was just going to put it to death, when the little suppliant implored his mercy, begging him not to stain his noble character with the blood of so small and insignificant a creature. The Lion, touched with compassion, instantly released his little trembling captive. Not long after, traversing the forest in search of his prey, he chanced to run into the toils of the hunters, and not being able to disengage himself, he set up a loud roar. The Mouse hearing the voice, and knowing it to be the Lion's, immediately repaired to the place, and bade him fear nothing, for that he was his friend. Instantly he fell to work, and with

2 L

his little sharp teeth gnawed asunder the knots and
fastenings of the toils, and set the royal brute at liberty.

APPLICATION.

THEY who generously shower benefits on their fellow-creatures, seldom fail of inspiring the great bulk
of them with a benevolent regard for their benefactors,
and often receive returns of kindness which they never
expected. Mercy is of all other virtues the most likely
to kindle gratitude in those to whom it is extended,
and it is difficult to find an instance of a conqueror
who ever had occasion to repent of his humanity and
clemency. The Fable gives us to understand, that
there is no person in the world so little, but even the
greatest may, at some time or other, stand in need of
his assistance; and consequently, it is good to shew favour, when there is room for it, towards those who
fall into our power. As the lowest people in life may,
upon occasion, be able either to serve or hurt us, it is
as much our interest as our duty to behave with good-
nature and lenity towards all with whom we have any
intercourse. A great soul is never so much delighted
as when an opportunity offers of making a return for
favours received; and a sensible man, however exalted
his station, will never consider himself secure from the
necessity of accepting a service from the poorest.

THE TORTOISE AND THE EAGLE.

A Tortoise, weary of his condition, by which he was confined to creep upon the ground, and ambitious to look about him with a larger prospect, proclaimed that if any bird would take him up into the air, and shew him the world, he would reward him with the discovery of an invaluable treasure, which he knew was hidden in a certain place of the earth. The Eagle accepted the offer, and having performed his undertaking, gently set the Tortoise again on the ground, and demanded the reward. The Tortoise was obliged to confess that he could not fulfil his promise, which he had made only with the view of having his fancy gratified. The Eagle, stung with resentment at being thus duped, grasped him again in his talons, and then soaring to a great height, let him fall, by which he was dashed to pieces.

APPLICATION.

MEN of honour are careful not to tarnish their reputations by falsifying their word, and always consider well how far it may be in their power to fulfil their promises before they make them.   They always strive to walk on the straight line of rectitude; and should they, in an unguarded moment, happen to stagger from it, they instantly retrace their steps, and feel unhappy until they have regained their station.   There is a simplicity in truth and virtue, which requires no artifices, and never leads us into difficulties, but points out the plain and safe way.   Deceit and cunning, on the contrary, involve those who practise them in a maze, and they are bewildered in their own falsehoods, from which no dexterity can extricate them.   The brain-racking schemes which villains practise to delude others, are commonly detected, and end in the unpitied punishment of themselves; for they seldom discover the folly of being wicked, until it has betrayed them into their ruin.   But such persons would do well to refresh their memories with the old adage which says, that " all knaves are fools, but all fools are not knaves."

THE POLECAT AND THE COCK.

A Polecat, that had long committed depredations
on the farm-yard, having a mind to make a meal of
the blood of the Cock, seized him one morning by surprize, and asked him what he could say for himself.
why slaughter should not pass upon him? The Cock
replied, that he was serviceable to mankind by crowing
in the morning, and calling them up to their daily labour. That is true, says the Polecat, and is the very
objection that I have against you, for you make such
a shrill impertinent noise, that people cannot sleep for
you. Besides, you are an incestuous rascal, and make
no scruple of lying with your mother and sisters.
Well, says the Cock, this I do not deny; but I do it
to procure eggs and chickens for my master. Ah!
villain, says the Polecat, hold your wicked tongue,

such impieties as these declare that you are no longer
fit to live.

APPLICATION.

WHEN a wicked man in power has a mind to glut
his appetite in any respect, innocence or even merit is
no protection against him. The cries of justice and
the voice of reason, are of no effect upon a conscience
hardened in iniquity, and a mind versed in a long
practice of wrong and robbery. Remonstrances, however reasonably urged, or movingly couched, have no
more influence upon the hearts of such, than the gentle evening breeze has upon the oak, when it whispers
among its branches; or the rising surges upon the
deaf rock, when they dash and break upon its sides.
Power should never be trusted in the hands of an impious selfish man, and one that has more regard to the
gratification of his own insatiable desires, than to public peace and justice; but as a wicked son may succeed
to the station of a virtuous and patriotic father, care
should be taken to guard against a surprise, by a vigilant watchfulness of the encroaching nature of power,
even when in benevolent hands, that those checks may
not be undermined which counteract its abuse in bad
ones. Had the poor Cock exerted his usual vigilance,
it would have served him much more effectually than
either his innocence or his eloquence.

THE FOWLER AND THE BLACKBIRD.

A Fowler was busy placing his nets, and putting his tackle in order, by the side of a coppice, when a Blackbird, who was perched on an adjacent tree, eyed him with great attention; but being at a loss to know the use of all this apparatus and preparation, had the curiosity to ask him what he was doing. I am, says the Fowler, building a fine city for you birds to live in, and providing it with meat and all manner of conveniences for you. Having said this, he departed and hid himself, and the Blackbird, believing his words, came into the nets and was taken; but when the man ran up to seize his captive, the Bird thus addressed him: If this be your faith, and these the cities you build, it will be a great pity if you should ever again persuade any poor simple bird to try to inhabit them.

APPLICATION.

THE fowler's professions of friendship for the birds, while he aimed at their destruction, may be paralleled by too many instances in real life; and however mortifying it may be to reflect upon, yet so it is, that the designing knave far too often succeeds in his deep-laid schemes to ensnare, over-reach, and ruin the honest and the unsuspecting man. Planners and projectors of this character, both of high and low degree, are suffered to roam at large, and it behoves the inexperienced to guard against their plots with a watchful eye; for while they smoothly disclaim taking any mean advantage over those they are addressing, with their plausible pretensions, their sole study and aim is to fill their own pockets, and then to hug themselves with the thoughts of their success, and to laugh at those whom they have duped. As long as people can be found credulous enough to suffer themselves to be imposed upon, so long will there arise gentry of this description, who will live in affluence by taking advantage of their weakness.

There will be sleeping enough in the Grave.

THE NURSE AND THE WOLF.

A Nurse, who was endeavouring to quiet a froward
child, among other things threatened to throw it out
of doors to the Wolf, if it did not leave off crying. A
Wolf, who chanced to be prowling near the door just
at the time, heard the expression, and believing the
woman to be in earnest, waited a long while about the
house, in expectation of having her words made good.
But at last the child, wearied with its own perverseness, fell asleep, and the Wolf was forced to return
back into the woods, empty and supperless. The Fox
meeting him, and surprized to see him going home so
thin and disconsolate, asked him what the matter was,
and how he came to speed no better that night? Ah!
do not ask me, says he, I was so silly as to believe
what the Nurse said, and have been disappointed.

APPLICATION.

MANY of the old moralists have interpreted this Fable as a caution never to trust a woman: a barbarous inference, which neither the obvious sense of the apologue, nor the disposition of the softer sex will warrant. For though some women may be fickle and unstable, yet the generality exceed their calumniators in truth and constancy, and have more frequently to complain of being the victims, than to be arraigned as the authors of broken vows. To us this Fable appears to mean little more than merely to shew how easily inclined we are, in all our various expectations through life, to delude ourselves into a belief of any thing which we desire to be true. The lover interprets every smile of his mistress in his own favour, and is then perhaps neglected. The beauty believes all mankind are dying for her, and is then deserted by her train of admirers. The followers of the great reckon a smile or a nod very auspicious omens, and deceive themselves with groundless hopes of employment or promotion, in expectation of which, they, like the Wolf at the Nurse's door, dangle away the time that might be usefully employed elsewhere, and at last are obliged to retire disappointed and hungry, crying out perhaps against the perfidy of those in power, instead of blaming their own sanguine credulity.

THE HARPER.

A Man who used to play upon the harp, and sing to it, in little ale-houses, and made a shift in those narrow confined walls to please the dull sots who heard him, from hence entertained an ambition of shewing his parts in the public theatre, where he fancied he could not fail of raising a great reputation and fortune in a very short time. He was accordingly admitted upon trial; but the spaciousness of the place, and the throng of the people, so deadened and weakened both his voice and instrument, that scarcely either of them could be heard, and where they could, his performance sounded so poor, so low, and wretched, in the ears of his refined audience, that he was universally hissed off the stage.

APPLICATION.

WHEN we are commended for our performances by people of much flattery or little judgment, we should be sure not to value ourselves upon it; for want of this caution, many a vain unthinking man has at once exposed himself to the censure of the world. A buffoon, though he would not be fit to open his mouth in a senate, or upon a subject where sound sense and a grave and serious behaviour are expected, may be very agreeable to a company disposed to be mirthful over a glass of wine. It is not the diverting a little, insignificant, injudicious audience or society, which can gain us a proper esteem, or insure our success, in a place which calls for a performance of the first rate. We should have either allowed abilities to please the most refined tastes, or judgment enough to know that we want them, and to have a care how we submit ourselves to the trial. And, if we have a mind to pursue a just and true ambition, it is not sufficient that we study barely to please; but it is of the greatest moment whom we please, and in what respect, otherwise we may not only lose our labour, but make ourselves ridiculous into the bargain.

THE ANT AND THE FLY.

In a dispute between the Ant and the Fly concerning precedency, the latter thus boasted: I have, said he, the uppermost seats at church, and even frequent the altars; I am taster to the gods, and a partaker of all their sacrifices; I am admitted into the palaces of kings, and enjoy myself at every entertainment provided for the princes of the earth, and all this without having occasion to labour. What have you to boast of, poor sorry drudge, crawling upon the earth, living in caverns and holes, and with constant exertion gathering up a grain of corn to support a wretched existence? Indeed! said the Ant, I pretend to none of these fine things. Visiting the great, and partaking of their festivals and sacrifices, might be entitled to some consideration, were you invited; but you are only an impudent intruder in such places. My time, indeed, is spent differently: I lead a life of industry,

which is crowned with health and vigour, and I am
constantly held up as an example of prudence and
foresight. I provide for present comforts and future
wants, and court not the favors, nor dread the frowns,
of any one ; while your laziness and vanity make you a
beggarly intruder wherever you hope to get a present
supply. You may, perhaps, sip honey one day, but on
the next you batten on carrion; and having propaga-
ted a numerous progeny, equally as noxious and useless as yourself, I then behold you from my comfortable, warm, well-stored mansion, in the winter of your
days, starving to death with hunger and cold.

APPLICATION.

THE worthless part of mankind, who pass through
the world without being of any service in it, and without acquiring the least reputation, seldom fail of adding empty pride to all their other failings, and behave
with arrogance towards those who contribute to the
comforts and happiness of society. They treat industrious persons as wretched drudges, appointed to labour for a poor subsistence, while they think themselves entitled to enjoy all the good things of this life,
though they of all others least deserve them. But the
worthy and industrious will generally find that the
pride and extravagance of these idle flies, bring them
at last to shame, if not to want, while their own honest
labours secure a good name, a happy mind, and a
sufficiency for their wants, if not a state of affluence.
In short, no one is a better gentleman than he whose
own honest industry supplies him with all necessaries,
and who pretends to no more acquaintance with honour than never to say or do a mean or an unjust thing.

THE MOUSE AND THE WEASEL.

A thin hungry Mouse, after much pushing and twisting, crept through a small hole, into a corn basket, where he gorged himself. so plentifully, that on his attempting to retire by the same passage, he found himself so swelled out, that, with all his endeavours, he could not squeeze through again. A Weasel, who stood at some distance, and had been diverting himself with the vain efforts of the little glutton, called to him sneeringly, Hark ye, Mr Mouse! remember that you were lean and half-starved when you got in at that small hole; and take my word for it, you must be as lean and half-starved before you can make your way out again.

APPLICATION.

THAT portion of mankind, whose inordinate desires push them on to stick at nothing in acquiring wealth, are seldom the most happy; for covetousness, which never produced one noble sentiment, often urges its votaries to break through the rules of justice, and then deprives them of the expected fruits of their iniquity. Besides great riches and care are almost inseparable; and there is often a quiet and content attending upon people of moderate circumstances, to which the wealthy man is an utter stranger. It has happened, even to monarchs, that their inroads on the possessions of others have tended to the detriment of the aggressor, who has been obliged to resign the rich spoils obtained by unjustifiable hostilities, and to refund the ill-gotten wealth, with a very bad grace: a punishment which Providence has wisely annexed to acts of violence and fraud, as the best security of the possessions of the just and virtuous, against the attempts of the wicked. Some men, from creeping in the lowest stations of life, have in process of time reached the greatest places, and grown so bulky by pursuing their insatiate appetite for money, that when they would have retired, they found themselves too opulent and full to get off. There has been no expedient for them to creep out, till they were squeezed and reduced in some measure to their primitive littleness. They that fill themselves with that which is the property of others, should always be so served before they are suffered to escape.

THE EAGLE AND THE FOX.

An Eagle that had young ones, looking for something to feed them with, happened to spy a Fox's Cub that lay basking itself abroad in the sun: she made a stoop, and trussed it immediately; but before she had carried it quite off, the old Fox coming home, implored her, with tears, to spare her Cub, and pity the distress of a poor fond mother, who would think no affliction so great as that of losing her child. The Eagle, whose nest was high in an old hollow tree, thought herself secure from all projects of revenge, and so bore away the Cub to her young ones, without shewing any regard to the supplications of the Fox. But that subtle creature, highly incensed at this outrageous barbarity, ran to an altar, where some country people had been sacrificing a kid in the open fields,

2 N

and catching up a fire-brand in her mouth, made towards the tree where the Eagle's nest was, with a resolution of revenge. She had scarcely reached its root, when the Eagle, terrified with the approaching ruin of herself and family, begged of the Fox to desist, and, with much submission, returned her the Cub safe and sound.

APPLICATION.

WHEN men in high situations happen to be wicked, how little scruple do they make of oppressing their poor neighbours ! They are perched upon a lofty station, and, having outgrown all feelings of humanity, are insensible to the pangs of remorse. The widow's tears, the orphan's cries, and the curses of the miserable, fall by the way, and never reach their hearts. But let such, in the midst of their flagrant injustice, remember how easy it is, notwithstanding their superior distance, for the meanest vassal to take his revenge. The bitterness of affliction (even where cunning is wanting) may animate the poorest spirit with desperate resolutions ; and when once the fury of revenge is thoroughly awakened, we know not what she may effect before she is lulled to rest again. The most powerful tyrants cannot prevent a resolved assassination : there are a thousand different ways for any private man to do the business, who is heartily disposed to it, and willing to satisfy his appetite for revenge, at the expence of his life. An old woman may clap a fire-brand to the palace of a prince, and a poor weak fool may destroy the children of the mighty.

THE BELLY AND THE MEMBERS.

In former days, it happened that the Members of the human body, taking some offence at the conduct of the Belly, resolved no longer to grant it the usual supplies. The Tongue first, in a seditious speech, aggravated their grievances; and after highly extolling the activity and diligence of the Hands and Feet, set forth how hard and unreasonable it was, that the fruits of their labour should be squandered away upon the insatiable cravings of a fat and indolent paunch. In short, it was resolved for the future to strike off his allowance, and let him shift for himself as well as he could. The Hands protested they would not lift a Finger to keep him from starving; and the Teeth refused to chew a single morsel more for his use. In this distress, the Belly remonstrated with them in vain; for during the clamour of passion the voice of reason is always disregarded. This unnatural resolution was kept as long as any thing of that kind can be kept, which was, until each of the rebel members pined away to the skin and bone, and could hold out no longer. Then they found there was no doing without the Belly, and, that idle and insatiable as it seemed, it contributed as much to the welfare of all the other parts, as they in their several stations did towards its maintenance.

APPLICATION.

This Fable was spoken by Menenius Agrippa, a Roman consul and general, when he was deputed by the senate to appease a dangerous tumult and insurrection of the people. The many wars the Romans were engaged in, and the frequent supplies they were obliged to raise, had so soured and inflamed the minds of the populace, that they were resolved to endure it no longer, and obstinately refused to pay the taxes. It is easy to discern how the great man applied this Fable: for, if the branches and members of a community refuse the government that aid which its necessities require, the whole must perish together. The rulers of a state, useless or frivolous as they may sometimes seem, are yet as necessary to be kept up and maintained in a proper and decent grandeur, as the family of each private person is, in a condition suitable to itself. Every man's enjoyment of that little which he gains by his daily labour, depends upon the government's being maintained in a condition to defend and secure him in the unmolested control and possession of it.

THE FATAL MARRIAGE.

A Mouse being ambitious of marrying into a noble family, paid his addresses to a young Lioness, and at length succeeded in entering into a treaty of marriage with her. When the day appointed for the nuptials arrived, the bridegroom set out in a transport of joy to meet his beloved bride; and coming up to her, passionately threw himself at her feet; but she, like a giddy thing as she was, not minding how she walked, accidentally set her foot upon her little spouse, and crushed him to death.

APPLICATION.

It is very unsafe for persons of low estate to form connections with those of a very superior situation. When wealthy persons of mean extraction and unre-

fined education, as an equivalent for their money, demand brides out of the nursery of the peerage, if they
should not be ruined by the giddy extravagance of
their high-born wives, their being despised, or at least
treated with neglect, is almost certain. But indeed,
much unhappiness follows the want of a sound judgment in the choice of a partner for life, whether it be
in high or low, rich or poor. No human contract is
of so important, as well as delicate a nature, as marriage. It is one of the grand epochs in the history of a man. It is an engagement which should be
voluntary, judicious, and disinterested, and can never be attended with honour, or blessed with happiness, if it has not its origin in mutual affection. If it
be either unsuitable or compulsory, it produces not
only individual misery, but consequences universally
pernicious. Sordid interest and vile dependence may
indeed sometimes act so powerfully, as to set nature
and true convenience aside, so as to make the yoke
which is jointly borne by the improper union of the high
and low, or by age and youth, put on an appearance
of regard for each other; but natural affection must
needs be wanting on one side or the other. Nature
has, however, with a strong hand, pointed out the path
to be pursued, and a few prudential rules only are necessary to keep us within it. If a man is of an unsound
constitution, or if he cannot provide for a family, let
him forbear matrimony: it is the duty of every man
who marries, to take a healthy woman for his wife, for
the sake of his children, and an amiable one, for his
own comfort. The same precaution ought to be taken
by the fair sex, unless they can make up their minds to
become nurses to tainted worn-out husbands, and their
puny nerveless offspring.

THE YOUNG MAN AND THE LION.

An opulent Old Man, who believed in omens and dreams, had an only Son, of whom he was dotingly fond. One night he dreamt that he saw the Young Man, while he was eagerly engaged in the chase, seized upon and torn in pieces by a Lion. This operated upon his fears to such a degree, that he instantly determined upon breaking off his Son's strong propensity to hunting, that he might be kept out of harm's way. For this purpose, he spared neither pains nor expence to make home agreeable to him. He had the rooms decorated with the finest paintings of forest scenery, and the hunting of wild beasts, with the reality of which the youth had been so much delighted; but the Young Man, debarred from his favourite pleasures, considered the palace a prison, and his father as the keeper. One day, when looking at the pictures, he cast his eye upon that of a Lion, and, enraged that he was confined for a dream about such a beast, he struck at the painting with his fist, with all his might. There happened to be a nail in the wall behind the canvas, which lacerated the hand terribly. The wound festered, and threw the Young Man into a fever, of which he died; so that the Father's dream was fulfilled by the very step he took to prevent it.

APPLICATION.

THOSE people who govern their lives by forebodings and dreams, and signs of ill-luck, are kept in a state of constant anxiety and uneasiness. Such a disposition is grounded on superstition, which is the offspring of a narrow mind, and adds greatly to the evils with which life is sufficiently loaded. Heaven has kindly concealed from us the knowledge of futurity, and it is therefore foolish for us to attempt to pry into it, or to disturb our minds with absurd conceptions of events which are only realised by our ridiculous precautions against them. How inconsistent is the conduct of people who imagine things to be predestined, and yet busy themselves in endeavours to prevent their coming to pass; as if the vain efforts of human power or prudence were able to counteract the will, or reverse the decrees of the Omnipotent.

THE KITE AND THE PIGEONS.

A Kite who had kept sailing in the air for many days near a dove-house, and made a stoop at several Pigeons to no purpose, for they were too nimble for him, at last had recourse to stratagem, and made a declaration to them, in which he set forth his own just and good intentions, and that he had nothing more at heart than the defence and protection of the Pigeons in their ancient rights and liberties, and how concerned he was at their unjust and unreasonable suspicions of himself, as if he intended by force of arms to break in upon their constitution, and erect a tyrannical government over them. To prevent all which, and thoroughly to quiet their minds, he thought proper to propose such terms of alliance, as might for ever cement a good understanding between them; one of which was, that they should accept of him for their

2 o

king, and invest him with all kingly privilege and pre-rogative over them; in return for which he promised them protection from all their enemies. The poor simple Pigeons consented: the Kite took the corona-tion oath, after a very solemn manner, on his part, and the Doves the oaths of allegiance and fidelity on theirs. But much time had not passed over their heads before the good ́Kite pretended that it was part of his prerogative to devour a Pigeon whenever he pleased; and this he was not contented to do himself only, but instructed the rest of the royal family in the same kingly arts. The Pigeons, reduced to this mise-rable condition, said one to the other, Ah! we de-serve no better! Why did we let him come in?

APPLICATION.

WHAT can this Fable be applied to, but the exceed-ing blindness and stupidity of that part of mankind, who wantonly and foolishly trust their native rights of liberty without good security? Who often chuse for guardians of their lives and fortunes, persons aban-doned to the most unsociable of vices; and seldom have any better excuse for such an error in politics, than that they were deceived in their expectation, or never thoroughly knew the manners of their king, till he had got them entirely in his power. We ought not to in-cur the possibility of being deceived in so important a matter as this; an unlimited power should not be trust-ed in the hands of any one who is not endowed with a perfection more than human.

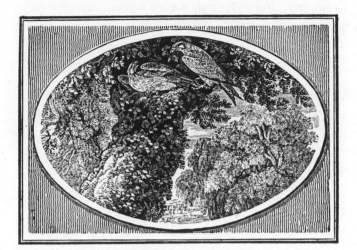

THE SICK KITE.

A Kite who had been sick a long time, beginning to be doubtful of recovery, begged of his Mother to go to all the churches and religious houses in the country, to try what prayers and offerings would effect in his behalf. The old Kite replied, Indeed, my dear son, I would willingly undertake any thing to save your life; but I have great reason to despair of doing you any service in the way you propose: for, with what face can I ask any thing of the Gods, in favour of one whose whole life has been a continued scene of rapine and injustice, and who has not scrupled, upon occasion, to rob even their altars?

APPLICATION.

THE rehearsal of this Fable almost unavoidably

draws our attention to that very serious and important point, the consideration of a death-bed repentance, the sincerity of which we may justly suspect in one whose whole life has been spent in acts of wickedness and im-- piety. To expose the absurdity of relying upon such a weak foundation, we need only ask the same question with the Kite in the Fable: how can he, who has offended the Gods all his life-time by acts of dishonour and injustice, expect that they will be pleased with him at last, for no other reason but because he fears he shall not be able to offend them any longer? Since the summons to " pass that bourn whence no traveller returns," must one day come, we ought always to be prepared to meet it. But when the whole life has been wasted, without communion with, or totally estranged from that Almighty Being, by whose fiat it was called into existence, then indeed the polluted soul must be distracted with the agonizing thoughts of appearing before Him, who created it for a very different purpose. Nothing but the consciousness of having led a virtuous life, can in the awful moment, disarm death of his terrors, and fortify the mind with cheering hopes and resignation. But this is a subject of the utmost importance, and the due enforcing of it is one of the most solemn duties of the pulpit.

THE FOX AND THE LION.

THE first time the Fox saw the Lion, he fell down at his feet, and was ready to die with fear. The second time he took courage, and could even bear to look upon him. The third time he had the impudence to come up to him, to salute him, and to enter into familiar conversation with him.

APPLICATION.

FROM this Fable we may observe the two extremes in which we may fail as to a proper behaviour towards our superiors. The one is a bashfulness, proceeding either from a vicious guilty mind, or a timorous rusticity; the other an over-bearing impudence, which assumes more than becomes it, and so renders the person insufferable to the conversation of well-bred reasonable

people. But there is a difference between the bashfulness which arises from a want of education, and the
shame-facedness that accompanies conscious guilt: the
first by time and a nearer acquaintance, may be ripened into a proper liberal behaviour; the other no sooner
finds an easy practicable access, but it throws off all
manner of reverence, grows every day more and more
familiar, and branches out at last into .the utmost in-
decency and irregularity. Indeed there are many occasions which may happen to cast an awe, or even a
terror, upon our minds at first view, without any just or
reasonable grounds; but upon a little recollection, or
a nearer insight, we recover ourselves, and can appear
indifferent and unconcerned, where before we were
ready to sink under a load of diffidence and fear. We
should upon such occasions use our endeavours to re-
gain a due degree of steadiness and resolution; but at
the same time we must have a care that our efforts in
that respect do not force the balance too much, and
make it rise to an unbecoming freedom, and an offensive familiarity.

THE DOG AND THE WOLF.

A Wolf in quest of prey, happened to fall in with a well-fed Mastiff. Ah, Tray, said he, one does not need to ask how you do, you look so plump and hearty. I wish I were as well provided for; but my gaunt looks shew that I fare very differently, although I dare say I venture my life ten times more than you do, in searching for a precarious subsistence, amidst woods and wilds, exposed to rain, and frost, and snow. If you will follow me, replies the Dog, and do as I do, I have no doubt you will change for the better, and soon be in as good plight as I am. The Wolf eagerly requested to be informed what would be required of him. Very little, replied the Mastiff; only drive away beggars, guard the master's house, caress him, and be submissive to his family, and you will be well fed and warmly lodged. To these conditions the Wolf had no objections; but as they were jogging along, he observed the hair worn off around the Dog's neck, and enquired the cause. O nothing, answered he, or a mere trifle; perhaps the collar, to which my chain is fastened, has left a mark. Chain! replied the Wolf, with some surprize; so then you are not permitted to go where and when you please? Not always, said Tray; but what does that signify? It signifies so much, rejoined the Wolf, that I am resolved to partake of no sumptuous fare with a chain about my neck; for half a meal, with liberty, is preferable to a full one without it.

APPLICATION.

TRUE greatness of soul will never give up liberty for any consideration whatever; for what are riches, grandeur, titles, or any other worldly good, if they are holden by so precarious a tenure as the arbitrary will of a tyrant! A mere competency, with liberty, is preferable to servitude amidst the greatest affluence; and even the lowest condition in life, with freedom, is better than the most exalted station without it. But liberty in a state of society does not consist in doing whatsoever we please; but only permits those actions by which we do no injustice to our neighbour, or to the community. The well-being of society requires the efforts of all, from the highest to the lowest, to preserve and support it; and since it appears to be the will of Omnipotence, that mankind should live in this state of social union (which does not admit of the unbridled freedom of the savage state) a certain portion of individual liberty must be given up for the good of the whole; but the sacrifice should be bounded by the common good: all beyond approaches towards slavery, and degrades the people who submit to it.

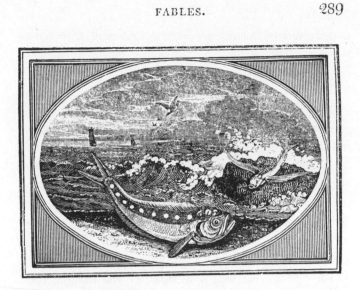

THE FLYING FISH AND THE DOLPHIN.

THE Flying Fish, to avoid its enemies, leaves the water, takes wing, and mounts up into the air. The Dolphin is one of the most constant of these enemies; and its velocity through the liquid element, it is said, surpasses that of every living creature, insomuch that as it darts along, the brilliancy and changeableness of its colours, which cannot be described, appear like the flash of a meteor. A Flying Fish being pursued by a Dolphin, in his eagerness to escape, took too long a flight, and his wings becoming dry, he fell upon a rock, where his death was inevitable. The Dolphin, in the keenness of his pursuit, ran himself on shore at the foot of the rock, and was left by the wave, gasping in the same condition as the other. Well, says the Flying Fish, I must die it is certain; but it is some

2 P

consolation to behold my merciless enemy involved in
the same fate.

APPLICATION.

WHEN brought low by a cruel and insolent oppress-
or, there is no torture we feel more poignantly, than
to see him triumphantly exulting in our downfal; and
the opposite extreme must take place in our minds, on
seeing our enemy over-shoot his mark, and in his turn
brought down to the same level of distress with ourselves.   The temper that is not touched with feelings
of this kind, must be of a highly philosophical cast indeed.   The great and powerful, for the sake of their
own peace of mind, should not unfeelingly persecute
their inferiors; for nothing is more sweet to some tempers, and scarcely any thing more easy to compass,
than revenge.

*It is not so ugly as a purse-proud,
ignorant, wicked man.*

THE LION AND THE FROG.

THE Lion hearing an odd kind of hollow voice, and seeing nobody, started up: he listened again, and hearing the noise repeated, he trembled and quaked for fear. At last, seeing a Frog crawl out of the lake, and finding that the noise he had heard was nothing but the croaking of that little creature, he went up to it with great anger; but checking himself, turned away from it, ashamed of his own timidity.

APPLICATION.

THE early prejudices of a wrong education can only be eradicated from the strongest minds. The weak retain them through life. This Fable is a pretty image of the vain fears and empty terrors, with which our weak misguided nature is so apt to be alarmed and disturbed. If we hear but ever so little noise which we

are not able to account for, immediately, nay, often
before we give ourselves time to consider about it, we
are struck with fear, and labour under a most unmanly
and unreasonable trepidation; more especially if the
alarm happens when we are alone, and in the dark.
These fears are ingrafted into our minds very early,
and therefore it is the more difficult, even when we are
grown up, and ashamed of them, to root them out of
our nature. They are chiefly the offspring of the nursery, and originate in the many terrific tales, and lying
stories, of those who have the management there; and
though every pains be afterwards taken to free the
mind from the impression of such groundless fears,
the weaker part of mankind are still apt to be terrified at the empty phantoms of ghosts, spectres, ap-
paritions, and hobgoblins. But whatever effect such
phantasies may have upon the guilty mind, innocence
has nothing to dread from supernatural causes. Fear
is however a natural passion, and its use is to put us
upon our guard against danger, by alarming the spirits; but it, like all our other passions, should be kept
in a state of subjection: for though they are all good
and useful servants, yet if once they get the better of
our reason, they prove the most domineering tyrants
imaginable; nor do any of them treat us in so abject
and slavish a manner as fear: it unnerves and enfeebles
our limbs, while it fetters our understandings; and at
the same time that it represents a danger near at hand,
disarms and makes us incapable of defending ourselves
from it. But we ought to call forth a sense of honour
and shame, to correct such weaknesses; and for this
purpose it will be useful to remember the Fable of the
Lion and the Frog.

THE KID AND THE WOLF.

A Kid being mounted upon the roof of a high shed,
and seeing a Wolf below, took the opportunity of af-
fronting him with the foulest reproaches: upon which
the Wolf looking up, replied, Do not value yourself,
vain creature, upon thinking you mortify me, for I
look upon this ill-language not as coming from you,
but from the place which protects you.

APPLICATION.

PLACE a coward out of the reach of danger, and
then no man can put on an appearance of greater
courage. In his castle he makes a great deal more
bluster and threatening than a man of spirit and honour would do, if placed in the same situation. A similar kind of overbearing behaviour too often shews

itself in the upstart worthless placeman, who taking advantage of his situation, which protects him, and knowing that he is out of the reach of our resentment, exhibits all the " insolence of office :" but such should be put in mind, that a saucy deportment is no sign of either courage, good sense, or good manners, and that a gentleman and a man of spirit will use no ill or unbecoming language to any person, however low in station.

THE COUNTRY AND THE CITY MOUSE.

A plain Country Mouse was one day unexpectedly visited at his hole, by a fine Mouse of the town, who had formerly been his play-fellow. The honest rustic, pleased with the honour, resolved to entertain his friend as sumptuously as possible. He set before him a reserve of delicate grey pease and bacon, a dish of fine oatmeal, some parings of new cheese, and to crown all with a dessert, a remnant of a charming mellow apple. When the repast was nearly finished, the spark of the town, taking breath, said, Old Crony, give me leave to be a little free with you; how can you bear to live in this melancholy hole here, with nothing but woods, and meadows, and mountains, and rivulets about you? Do you not prefer the conversation of the world to the chirping of birds, and the splendour of the court, to the rude aspect of a wild like this? With many flowery arguments, he at last prevailed upon his country friend to accompany him to town, and about midnight they safely entered a certain great house, where there had been an entertainment the day before. Here it was the courtier's turn to entertain, and placing his guest on a rich Persian carpet, they both began to regale most deliciously, when on a sudden the noise of somebody opening the door, made them scuttle in confusion about the dining-room. The rustic in particular was ready to die with fear at the many hair-breadth escapes which followed. At last, recovering himself, Well, says he, if this be your town-life, much good may it do you. Give me my poor quiet hole again, with my homely, but comfortable grey pease.

APPLICATION.

A moderate fortune, with a quiet retirement in the country, is preferable to the greatest affluence, attended with the care and the perplexity of business. How often are we deceived by the specious shows of splendour and magnificence; and what a poor exchange does he make, who gives up ease and content in an humble situation, to engage in difficulties, and encounter perils in affluence and luxury! The ploughman in the field, who labours for his daily pittance, earns his bread with less uneasiness and fatigue, than the man who haunts levees to obtain wealth and preferment. Riches, properly used, are indeed very conducive to ease and happiness; but if we leave any comfortable situation to procure them, or abuse the possession of them by riot and intemperance, we resign the end for the means, mistake the shadow for the substance, and convert the instruments of good fortune into the engines of anxiety and solicitude.

THE ONE-EYED DOE.

A Doe that had lost an eye, used to graze near the sea; and that she might be the more secure from harm, she kept her blind side towards the water, from whence she had no apprehension of danger, and with the other surveyed the country as she fed. By this vigilance and precaution, she thought herself in the utmost security; but a sly fellow, with two poaching companions, who had watched her several days to no purpose, at last took a boat, and came gently down upon her, and shot her. The Doe, in the agonies of death, breathed out this doleful complaint: O hard fate, that I should receive my death's wound from the side whence I expected no ill, and be safe in that quarter where I looked for the most danger.

2 Q

APPLICATION.

We are liable to many misfortunes that no care or foresight can prevent; but we ought to provide in the best way we can against them, and leave the rest to Providence. The wisest of men have their foibles or blind sides, and have their enemies too, who watch to take advantage of their weaknesses. It behoves us therefore to look to ourselves on the blind side, as the part that lies most exposed to an attack. Vigilance and caution are commonly our best preservatives from evil, and security is often a fatal enemy, when we cherish it so as to lull all our apprehensions to rest. We should not however encourage in ourselves the slavish principle of fear, nor make ourselves miserable on account of latent evils, which it is not in our power to prevent. The ways and workings of Providence are inscrutable; and it is not in the power of human prudence to obviate all the accidents of life.

THE TREES AND THE WOODMAN.

A Countryman being in want of a handle for his hatchet, entered a wood and looked among the branches for one that would suit his purpose. The Trees, with a curiosity natural to some other creatures, asked him what he was seeking? He replied that he only wanted a piece of wood to make a handle to his axe, and begged they would be so good as to permit him to serve himself. Since that is all, said the Trees, help yourself, and welcome. He immediately availed himself of the permission, and had no sooner fitted up his instrument, than he began pell-mell to cut and hack about him, felling the noblest trees in all the forest, without distinction. The Oak is said to have spoke thus to the Beech, in a low whisper: Brother, we must take all this for our easy credulity, and imprudent generosity.

2 Q 2

APPLICATION.

ONE would imagine that the natural principle of self-preservation implanted in us, would make it unnecessary to caution any one not to furnish an enemy with arms against himself. Yet daily experience shews us that such instances of imprudence are not uncommon. In this life we are liable to be surrounded with calamities and distresses: we should therefore be cautious of adding to our misfortunes, by our own want of caution, and of putting power into the hands of those enemies, which our merit or our affluence may tempt to rise up against us. Any person in a community, by what name or title soever distinguished, who affects a power which may possibly hurt a people, is their enemy, and therefore they ought not to trust him: for though he were ever so fully determined not to abuse such a power, yet he is so far a bad man, as he disturbs a nation's quiet, and makes them jealous and uneasy, by desiring to have it, or even retaining it, when it may prove mischievous. If we consult history, we shall find that the thing called prerogative, has been claimed and contended for chiefly by those who never intended to make a good use of it; and as readily resigned by wise and just princes, who had the true interest of their people at heart. How like senseless stocks do they act, who, by complimenting some capricious mortal, from time to time, with scraps of prerogative, at last put it out of their power to maintain their just and natural liberty !

THE EAGLE AND THE CROW.

An Eagle flew down from the top of a high rock, and making a stoop at a Lamb, seized it with her strong talons, and bore aloft her bleating prize to her young. A Crow observing what passed, was ambitious of performing the same exploit, and darted down upon a Ram; but instead of being able to carry it up into the air, she found she had got her claws entangled in its fleece, and could neither move herself nor her fancied prize. Thus fixed, she was soon taken by the Shepherd, and given away to some boys, who eagerly enquired what bird it was? An hour ago, said he, she fancied herself an Eagle; however I suppose she is by this time convinced that she is but a Crow.

APPLICATION.

It is impossible for any man to take a true measure

of the abilities of another, without an exact knowledge and true judgment of his own; a false estimate of
which always exposes him to ridicule, and sometimes
to danger.   Every man ought therefore to examine the
strength of his own mind with attention and impar-
tiality, and not fondly to flatter himself that he can by
an awkward and ill-judged emulation soar to the height
which has been attained by men endowed by nature
with great abilities and original talents, matured by
industry.   We can no more adopt the genius of another man, than we can assume his shape and person.
The bright original in every department of the arts
and sciences will be valued and esteemed, whilst his
puny imitators will be treated with neglect, or be despised.   Almost every man has something original in
himself, which, if duly cultivated, might perhaps procure him respect and applause, and it is creditable for
him to endeavour justly to obtain them.

THE HORSE AND THE STAG.

In ancient times, when the Horse and the Deer ranged the forest with uncontrolled freedom, it happened that contentions arose between them about grazing in particular meadows. These disputes ended in a conflict between them, in which the Deer proved victorious, and with his sharp horns drove the Horse from the pasture. Full of disappointment and chagrin, the Horse applied to the Man, and craved his assistance, in order to re-establish him in the possession of his rights. The request was granted, on condition that he would suffer himself to be bridled, saddled, and mounted by his new ally, with whose assistance he entirely defeated his enemy; but the poor Horse was mightily disappointed when, upon returning thanks to the Man, and desiring to be dismissed, he received this answer: No, I never knew before how useful a drudge you were; now I have found what you are good for, you may be assured I will keep you to it.

APPLICATION.

VICTORIES may be purchased at too dear a rate, if we solicit the assistance of allies capable of becoming our most formidable enemies, and it will be vain to flatter ourselves, that the yoke of slavery, if we once willingly suffer it to be laid upon our shoulders, can be easily shaken off, when the ends for which we bore it are accomplished. The Fable is intended to caution us against consenting to any thing that might prejudice public liberty, as well as to keep us upon our guard in the preservation of that which is of a private nature. This is the use and interpretation given of it by Horace, one of the best and most polite philosophers that ever wrote. After reciting the Fable, he applies it thus: This, says he, is the case of him, who, dreading poverty, parts with that invaluable jewel, liberty, like a wretch as he is, he will always be subject to a tyrant of some sort or another, and be a slave for ever, because his avaricious spirit knew not how to be contented with that moderate competency, which he might have possessed independent of all the world.

THE MILLER, HIS SON, AND THEIR ASS.

A Miller and his Son were taking their Ass to market to sell him, and that he might get thither in good condition, they drove him gently before them. They had not proceeded far before they met a company of travellers: Sure, say they, you are mighty careful of your Ass; one of you might as well get up and ride, as suffer him to walk on at his ease, while you trudge after on foot. In compliance with this advice, the Old Man set his Son upon the beast. And now, they had scarcely advanced a quarter of a mile further, before they met another company. You idle young rogue, said one, why dont you get down, and let your poor father ride? Upon this, the Old Man made his Son dismount, and got up himself. While they were marching in this manner, a third company began to insult the father. You hard-hearted wretch, say they, how can you suffer that poor lad to wade through the dirt, while you, like an alderman, ride at your ease? The good-natured Miller stood corrected, and immediately took his Son up behind him. And now the next man they met exclaimed, with more vehemence and indignation than all the rest, Was there ever such a couple of lazy loobies! to overload in so unconscionable a manner, a poor dumb creature, who is far less able to carry you, than you are to carry him! The complying Old Man would have been half inclined to make the trial, had not experience by this time sufficiently convinced him, that there cannot be a more fruitless attempt, than to endeavour to please all mankind.

APPLICATION.

It is better to pursue the dictates of one's own reason, than attempt to please every body; for to do this is next to impossible. Therefore we ought to decide according to the best of our judgment, and correct our mistakes from our own experience. Wise men are instructed by reason; men of less understanding by experience; the most ignorant by necessity; and beasts by instinct. When a man so neglects himself, as not to make a just use of his reason and his mental powers, in combating with prejudice and folly, as well as the caprice of others, he will ever be led on in a maze of error, wavering and embarrassed about pursuing this or that path, until between them he is lost in a labyrinth, from which he will never be able to extricate himself as long as he lives.

THE ANT AND THE GRASSHOPPER.

A commonwealth of Ants, having, after a busy summer, provided every thing for their wants in the winter, were about shutting themselves up for that dreary season, when a Grasshopper in great distress, and in dread of perishing with cold and hunger, approached their avenues, and with great humility begged they would relieve his wants, and permit him to take shelter in any corner of their comfortable mansion.   One of the Ants asked him how he had disposed of his time in summer, that he had not taken pains and laid in a stock, as they had done?   Alas! my friends, says he, I passed away the time merrily and pleasantly, in drinking, singing, and dancing, and never once thought of winter.   If that be the case, replied the Ant, all I have to say is this: that they who drink, sing, and dance in the summer, run a great risk of starving in the winter.

APPLICATION.

As summer is the season in which the industrious
laborious husbandman lays up his supplies for the winter, so youth and manhood are the times of life which
we should employ in laying in such a stock as may
suffice for helpless old age; yet there are many whom
we call rational creatures, who squander away in a
profuse prodigality, whatever they get in their younger
days, as if the infirmity of age would require no supplies to support it, or at least would find them admi-
nistered to it in some miraculous way. From this Fable we learn this admirable lesson, never to lose the
present opportunity of fairly and honestly providing
against the future evils and accidents of life; and while
health and the vigour of our faculties remain firm and
entire, to lay them out to the best advantage; so that
when age and infirmities despoil us of our strength and
abilities, we may not have to bewail that we have neglected to provide for the wants of our latter days: for it
should always be remembered, that " a youth of revels
breeds an age of care," and that temperance in youth
lays the foundation of health and comfort for old age.

THE HORSE AND THE LION.

An old Lion, finding that many of the beasts had become too nimble for him, and that he could not come at his prey so readily as before, craftily gave out that he had long studied physic and surgery in foreign countries, and that he could cure every kind of disorder to which the beasts were liable. These professions having been spread abroad, he hoped to get many of the animals to come within his clutches. The Horse seeing through the whole of the scheme, was resolved to be even with him; and so humouring the thing as if he suspected nothing, he feigned himself to be in great pain from a wound in his foot, and limping up to the Lion, he begged he would examine the part and administer relief. The Lion, though intent only upon making a good meal of horse-flesh, begged the Horse to hold up his foot that he might see it: this was no sooner done, than the Horse gave him so violent a blow on the nose, as quite stunned him, and scampered off, neighing at the success of a trick, which had defeated the purpose of one who intended to have tricked him out of his life.

APPLICATION.

WE ought never to put trust in the fair words and pretensions of those who have both an interest and inclination to ruin us; and where we find foul play thus intended against us, it is not in the nature of things to expect that we should not, if we can, turn the tables upon the plotters. Treachery has something so wicked and worthy of punishment in its nature, that it deserves to meet with a return of its own kind. An open revenge is too liberal for it, and nothing matches it but itself. Though a man of sense and honour will always view tricking and fraud of all kinds as mean and beneath him, and will despise setting such an example, yet it cannot be inconsistent with virtue to counteract the schemes of those who are taking all manner of undue advantages, and hatching wicked plots to undermine us.

THE FOX IN THE WELL.

A Fox having fallen into a well, made a shift, by sticking his claws into the sides, to keep his head above water. Soon after, a Wolf came and peeped over the brink, to whom the Fox applied, and very earnestly implored his assistance to help him out, or he should be lost. Ah! poor Reynard, says he, I pity your misfortune; poor creature, I am sorry for you with all my heart: how did you happen to slip into this well? pray how long have you been in this melancholy situation? Nay, I prithee friend, replies the Fox, if you wish me well, do not stand pitying me, but lend me some succour as soon as you can; for pity is but cold comfort when one is up to the chin in water, and within a hair's breadth of starving or drowning.

APPLICATION.

If we would really manifest our sorrow for the sufferings of another, let our pity be shewn by our friendly endeavours to relieve him; for indeed pity of itself is but poor comfort at any time, unless it produces something more substantial. If we cannot do this, let us not offend the sensibility, and add to the anguish of a delicate mind, by empty professions and unmeaning compassion. For, to stand bemoaning the misfortunes of our friends, without offering some expedient to alleviate them, is only echoing their grief, and putting them in mind that they are miserable. He is truly my friend, who with a ready presence of mind supports me; not he who merely condoles with me upon my ill success, and expresses his sorrow for my mishap.

THE GARDENER AND HIS DOG.

A Gardener's Dog happened by some mischance to fall into the well: his Master ran immediately to his assistance; but when helping him out, the surly brute bit his hand. The Gardener took this ungrateful treatment so ill, that he shook him off, and left him to shift for himself. Thou wicked wretch! said he, to injure the hand that was stretched forth to save thy life! The hand of thy Master, who has hitherto fed and taken care of thee! Die there as thou deservest; for so base and unnatural a creature is not fit to live.

APPLICATION.

WHEN a man has suffered his mind to become so debased as to be capable to doing injuries to him who has showered benefits on his head, he can scarcely be treated with too much severity. He deserves at least to be scouted as an outcast to society. All the favours that are bestowed upon men of this worthless disposition, are thrown away; for the envy and malevolence of the ingrate, work him up into a hatred of his benefactor. Generous men should therefore use a just circumspection in the choice of the objects of their benevolence, before they give way to the feelings of the heart, or waste its bountiful overflowings upon those who, instead of making a grateful return, will bite them like a drowning but spiteful dog. The Fable is also intended as an admonition to servants, who owe an especial duty to their masters; whose kindness should be met by their faithful exertions to serve them; and whose interest they ever ought to make their own.

THE DEER AND THE LION.

A Deer, terrified by the cry of the Hunters, instead of trusting to his fleetness, made towards a cave which he chanced to espy, and in which he hoped to conceal himself until they were passed by; but he had scarcely reached the entrance before he was seized by a Lion who lay crouching there, ready to spring upon his prey, and who instantly killed and tore him to pieces. In the last agonies of death, he thus gave vent to his feelings: Ah, me! said he, unhappy creature that I am. I hoped in this cave to escape the pursuit of men; but have fallen into the jaws of the most cruel and rapacious of wild beasts.

APPLICATION.

THIS Fable points out the dangers to which we ex-

2 s 2

pose ourselves, when, for want of presence of mind, we suffer ourselves to be guided by our unreasoning fears, which no sooner shew us an evil, than they throw us into the utmost confusion in our manner of escaping, and prevent us from discerning the safe path by which we ought to avoid it. Thus, in a rash endeavour to shun a less danger, we oftentimes blindly run headlong into a greater. The fate of the Deer should warn us to consider well what may be the ultimate consequences, before we take any important step; for many paths which appear smooth and pleasant at a distance, are found to be rough and dangerous, when we come to tread them; and many a plausible scheme, which promises us ease and safety, is no better than a tempting bower, with a Lion crouching among its foliage, ready to spring upon and devour us.

THE PLOUGHMAN AND FORTUNE.

As a Ploughman was turning up the soil, his plough uncovered a treasure which had been hidden there. Transported with joy, he seized upon it, and fervently began to thank the ground for being so liberal to him. Fortune passing by, observed what he was about, and could not forbear shewing her resentment at it. You stupid creature, said she, to lie thus thanking the ground, and take no notice of me! If you had lost such a treasure, instead of finding one, I should have been the first you would have laid the blame upon.

APPLICATION.

How often do we ascribe our success or misfortunes to wrong causes! Vanity sometimes leads us to consider our prosperity as the natural result of our own

sagacity, and inattention sometimes induces us to make
acknowledgments to wrong persons.   But if we would
have our praises valued, we should be cautious to direct
them properly.   Our thanks are an indirect affront to
those who receive them without deserving them; and
at the same time an act of open ingratitude to those
who merit them without receiving them.   In prosperity, as well as in adversity, let us not forget the power
and goodness of Heaven; and if we implore the aid of
the Almighty in our distress, we should not neglect to
send up our acknowledgments of his goodness with the
voice of gratitude.

THE APE AND THE FOX.

An Ape meeting with a Fox, humbly requested he would be so good as to give him some of the superfluous hair from his bushy tail, to make into a covering for his bare posteriors, which were exposed to all the inclemency of the weather; and he endeavoured to further his suit by observing to Reynard, that he had far more than he had any occasion for, and a great part even dragged along in the dirt. The Fox answered, that as to his having too much, it was more than he knew; but be it as it would, he had rather sweep the ground with his tail as long as he lived, than part with the least bit of it for a covering to the filthy posteriors of an Ape.

APPLICATION.

Riches, in the hands of a wise and generous man,

are a blessing to the community in which he lives: they are like the light and the rain, and diffuse a good all around them. But wealth, when it falls to the lot of those who want benevolence and humanity, serves only as an instrument of mischief, or at best produces no advantage to the rest of mankind. The good man considers himself as a kind of steward to those from whom fortune has withheld her smiles, and thus shews his gratitude to Heaven for the abundance which has been showered down upon him. He directs the superfluous part of his wealth at least, to the necessities of such of his fellow-creatures as are worthy of it, and this he would do from feeling, though there were no religion which enjoined it. But selfish avaricious persons, who are generally knaves, how much soever they may have, will never think they have enough, much less be induced, by any consideration of virtue or religion, to part with any portion for the purposes of charity and beneficence. If the riches and power of the world were to be always in the hands of the virtuous part of mankind, it would seem, according to our human conceptions, that they would produce more good than in those of the vile and grovelling mortals, who often possess them. Without any merit, these move apparently in a sphere of ease and splendour, while good sense and honesty have to struggle in adversity, or walk in the dirt. But the all-wise Disposer of Events does certainly permit this order of things for just, good, and wise purposes, though our shallow understandings are not able to fathom them.

THE THIEF AND THE BOY.

An arch mischievous Boy, sitting by the side of a well, observed a noted Thief coming towards him. The little dissembler, wiping his eyes, affected to be in great distress. The Thief asking him what was the matter? ah! says the Boy, I shall be severely flogged, for in attempting to get some water, I have dropped the silver tankard into the well. Upon this the Thief, eager for a prize, stripped off his cloaths, and went down to the bottom to search for it; where having groped about to no purpose, he came up again, but found neither the Boy nor the cloaths, the little wag having run off with and hidden them, and left the Thief to look for the tankard at his leisure.

2 T

APPLICATION.

NOTHING gives more entertainment to honest men,
than to see rogues and sharpers tricked and punished
in the pursuit of their schemes of villainy, by making
their own contrivances instrumental in bringing down
their wickedness upon their own heads.   In these instances, Justice seems as it were to be acting in person, and saves the trouble of publicly enforcing punishment by the penal laws; but indeed vice carries with
it its own punishment, and the misery attendant upon
it in this world, seems always pretty exactly balanced
to its various degrees of enormity.   The abandoned
man drags on a contemptible or infamous life, with a
constantly deadened or disturbed conscience, and a-
midst associates like himself, where he can never hope
to meet with either friendship or fidelity.

THE FOX AND THE SICK LION.

IT was reported that the Lion was sick, and the beasts were given to understand that they could not make their court better than by going to visit him. Upon this they generally went; but it was particularly taken notice of, that the Fox was not one of the number. The Lion therefore dispatched one of his Jackalls to enquire why he had so little charity and respect as never to come near him, at a time when he lay so dangerously ill, and every body else had been to see him? Why, replies the Fox, pray present my duty to his majesty, and tell him that I have the same respect for him as ever, and have been coming several times, but was fearful of being troublesome, as I have observed, from the prints of their footsteps, that great numbers have gone into the royal den; but I have not seen a single trace of their coming out again.

APPLICATION.

He that embarks implicitly in any scheme, may be mistaken, notwithstanding the number who keep him company; but he that keeps out till he sees reason to enter, acts upon true maxims of policy; and it is the quintessence of prudence not to be too easy of belief: for a rash and hasty credulity has been the ruin of many. Men who habituate themselves to think, will profit by the experience of others, as well as their own: but commonly the multitude do not reason, but stupidly follow each other step by step; not moving out of the sphere in which chance has placed them: and the notions or prejudices they may have imbibed in youth, remain with them to the last. There is no opinion, however impious or absurd, that has not its advocates in some quarter of the world. Whoever, therefore, takes up his creed upon trust, and grounds his principles on no better reason than his being a native or inhabitant of the regions wherein they prevail, becomes a disciple of Mahomet in Turkey, and of Confucius in China; a Jew, or a Pagan, as the accident of birth decides.

THE SUN AND THE WIND.

A dispute arose between the North Wind and the Sun, about the superiority of their power, and they agreed to determine matters by trying which of them could first compel a Traveller to throw off his cloak. The North Wind began, and blew a very cold blast, accompanied by a sharp driving shower; but this, and whatever else he could do, instead of making the Man quit his cloak, induced him to gird it about him more closely. Next came the Sun, who, breaking out from a cloud, drove away the cold vapours, and darted his warm sultry beams upon the weather-beaten Traveller. The Man growing faint with the heat, first threw off his heavy cloak, and then flew for protection to the shade of a neighbouring grove.

APPLICATION.

THERE is something in the temper of man so averse
to severe and boisterous treatment, that he who endeavours to carry his point in that way, instead of prevailing, generally leaves the mind of him whom he has
thus attempted to subdue, in a more confirmed and
obstinate state. Bitter words and hard usage freeze
the heart into an obduracy, which mild, persuasive,
and gentle language only can dissolve. Persecution
has always fixed those opinions which it was intended
to dispel; and the quick growth of christianity in early
times, is attributed in a great measure to the barbarous
reception which its first teachers met with in the Pagan world; and since that time the different modes of
faith which have grown out of christianity itself, have
been each established by the same kind of intolerant
spirit. To reflect upon these things, furnishes matter
of wonder and regret, for the benevolent Author of the
christian religion taught neither intolerance nor persecution. The doctrines he laid down are plain, pure,
and simple. They teach mercy to the contrite, aid to
the humble, and eternal happiness to the good. In
short, persecution is the scandal of all religion, and
like the north wind in the Fable, only tends to make
a man wrap his notions more closely about him.

THE HORSE AND THE ASS.

THE Horse, adorned with his great war-saddle, and champing his foaming bridle, came thundering along the high-way, and made the mountains echo with his neighing. He had not gone far before he overtook an Ass, who was labouring under a heavy burthen, and moving slowly on in the same track. In an imperious tone he threatened to trample him in the dirt, if he did not get out of the way. The poor Ass, not daring to dispute, quietly got aside as fast as he could, and let him go by. Not long after this, the same Horse, in an engagement, happened to be shot in the eye, which made him unfit for show, or any military business, so he was stripped of his ornaments, and sold to a carrier. The Ass meeting him in this forlorn condition, thought that now it was his time to retort:

Hey-day, .friend, says he, is it you! Well, I always believed that pride of your's would one day have a fall.

APPLICATION.

It is an affectation of appearing considerable, that puts men upon being proud and insolent; but this very affectation infallibly makes them appear little and despicable in the eyes of discerning people. Did the proud man but rightly consider what kind of ingredients pride is composed of and fed with, and the unstable foundation, and the tottering pinnacle upon which it stands, he would blush at the thoughts of it, and cease to be puffed up by the little supernumerary advantages, whether of birth, fortune, or title, which he may enjoy above his neighbours. These might indeed be a blessing to him, and to the community in which he lives, if wisely used; but if guided by pride, and consequently by want of sense, they will prove only a curse; and the reverence and respect which he looks for, will not be paid with sincerity, nor does he deserve it; and should the tide of misfortune set in against him, instead of friendship and commiseration, he will meet with nothing but contempt, and that with much more justice than ever he himself expressed it towards others. The vain proud man ought to be put in mind, that the time is not far distant, when his skull will not be distinguished from that of the beggar; and that there is no state, however exalted, so permanent, that it may not be reduced to a level with the lowest.

THE HAWK AND THE FARMER.

A Hawk, in the eagerness of his pursuit after a Pigeon, flew with such violence against the corner of a hedge, that he was stunned and fell. A Farmer, who had been looking about his fields, saw the whole transaction, and instantly ran and picked up the Hawk, and was going to kill him; but the latter begged the Man would let him go, assuring him he was only following a Pigeon, and neither intending, nor had done, any harm to him. To which the Farmer replied, and what harm had the Pigeon done to you? and wrung his head off immediately.

APPLICATION.

In all our transactions through life, to suppose ourselves in the place of those we may be dealing

2 U

with, will be the most certain check upon our own
conduct; and we ought always to consult our conscience about the rectitude of our behaviour: for this
we may be assured of, that we are acting wrong, whenever we are doing any thing to another, which we
should think unjust, if it were done to us.   Let those,
therefore, who intend to act justly, but take this view
of things, and all will be well.   There will be no danger of their oppressing others, or fear of their falling
into error or danger themselves.   Nothing but an habitual inadvertency as to this particular, can be the
occasion of so many ingenuous noble spirits being so
often engaged in courses opposite to virtue and honour.

THE FOX AND THE COUNTRYMAN.

A Fox being closely pursued by the Hunters, and almost run down, begged of a Countryman to give him protection, and save his life. The Man consented, and pointed out a hovel, into which the Fox crept, and covered himself up among some straw. Presently up came the Hunters, and enquired of the Man if he had seen the Fox, and which way he had taken? No, said he, I have not seen him here, he has passed another way; but all the while he nodded with his head, and pointed with his finger to the place where the Fox was hidden. These signals the Hunters, in the eagerness of pursuit, did not notice, but calling off the dogs, they dashed along in another direction. Soon after, the Fox came out of his hiding-place, and was sneaking off, when the Man calling after him,—Hollo, says he, is this the way you behave then, to go without

2 u 2

thanking the benefactor who has saved your life? Reynard, who had peeped all the while, and had seen what passed, answered, I know what obligation I owe you well enough, and I assure you if your actions had agreed with your words, I should have endeavoured, however incapable of it, to have returned you suitable thanks.

APPLICATION.

DISSIMULATION and double dealing are among the most odious vices, and a hollow friend is worse than an open enemy; for in the full confidence of friendship, we are led to depend upon the man who uses that confidence to betray us. To pretend to keep another's council, and appear in his interest, while underhand we are giving intelligence to his enemies, is treacherous, knavish, and base. Truth is a plain and open virtue, and cannot be practised in part; and truth and sincerity are the same; wherefore he that equivocates and adheres to his promise in one sense, without preserving it inviolably in its full extent and meaning, departs as much from truth and sincerity as the most direct liar.

" And be those juggling friends no more believ'd,
" That palter with us in a double sense;
" That keep the word of promise to the ear,
" And break it to our hope."

ÆSOP AT PLAY.

An Athenian one day found Æsop entertaining himself with a company of little Boys at their childish diversions, and began to jeer and laugh at him for it. Æsop, who was too much a wag himself to suffer others to ridicule him, took a bow unstrung, and laid it upon the ground. Then calling the censorious Athenian, Now philosopher, says he, expound the riddle if you can, and tell us what the unstrained bow implies. The Man, after racking his brains a considerable time to no purpose, at last gave it up, and declared he knew not what to make of it. Why, says Æsop, smiling, if you keep a bow always bent, it will lose its elasticity presently; but if you let it go slack, it will be fitter for use when you want it.

APPLICATION.

THE mind of man is not formed for unremitted attention, nor his body for uninterrupted labour; and both are in this respect like a bow. We cannot go through any business requiring intense thought, without unbending the mind, any more than we can perform a long journey without refreshing ourselves by due rest at the several stages of it. Continual labour, as in the case of the bended bow, destroys the elasticity and energy of both body and mind. It is, therefore, absolutely necessary for the studious man to unbend, and the laborious one to take his rest, or both lose their tone and vigour, and become dull and languid. It is to remedy these extremes, that pastimes and diversions ought to be kept up, provided they are innocent. The heart that never tastes of pleasure, shuts up, grows stiff, and is at last incapable of enjoyment.

THE FOX AND THE WOLF.

THE Wolf having laid in a store of provisions, snug-
ly kept in his den, and indulged himself in feasting
upon them.   The Fox observing this seclusion of the
Wolf, became inquisitive to know the cause, and by
way of satisfying his curiosity and his suspicions, he
went and paid the Wolf a visit.   The latter excused
himself from seeing the Fox, by pretending he was
very much indisposed.   The Fox having smelt how
matters stood, took his leave, and immediately went
to a Shepherd to inform him of the discovery he had
made, and that he had nothing else to do but to take
a good weapon with him, and with it easily dispatch
the Wolf as he lay dosing in his cave.   The Shepherd
following his directions, presently went and killed the
Wolf.   The wicked Fox then slily took possession
of the cave and the provisions to himself; but he did

not enjoy them long, for the same Shepherd shortly afterwards passing by the place, and seeing the Fox there, dispatched him also.

APPLICATION.

A villain, whose only aim is to get what he can, will as soon betray the innocent as the guilty. Let him but know where there is a suspected person, and propose a reward, and he will seldom fail to work the suspicion up to high treason, and will be at no loss to produce sufficient proofs of it. Men of this stamp will not be content with practising one single villainy; for having never laid down any good principles for their guide, they will go on triumphantly in their wickedness for a time, and though, perhaps, they may be the instruments of bringing other villains to punishment, yet they will at last suffer in their turn; for, after being detested by all good men, justice will, sooner or later, overtake their crimes, and hurl down its vengeance on their heads, with a measure equal at least to the sufferings their perfidy has occasioned to others. The fate of such wretches can never excite the smallest commiseration; for no character is so truly detestable, as that of a spy and informer.

THE RAVEN AND THE SERPENT.

A Raven in quest of food, seeing a Serpent basking in the sun, soused down, seized it with his horny beak, and attempted to carry it off. But the Serpent, writhing with the pain, twisted its elastic coils so firmly about the Raven, and bit him with such envenomed fierceness, that he fell to the ground mortally wounded. In the agonies of death, the Raven confessed this was a just punishment upon him, for having attempted to satisfy his greedy appetite at the expence of another's welfare.

APPLICATION.

WHEN men suffer their passions to set aside their reason, they soon become sensual in their appetites, and inordinate in their desires. Moral rectitude takes its departure from their minds, and led by their evil spirit, they soon become fitted for the commission of any enormity. They give the rein to their unbridled lusts, and regardless of consequences, stop at nothing to gratify their brutal desires. But if we mark the progress of such men through life, it will be found that, besides losing the great and virtuous pleasures of self-approbation, and incurring the stings of a guilty conscience, their wicked career often meets just punishment from retaliations in kind, which the objects of their iniquitous proceedings unexpectedly retort upon them.

Waiting for Death

THE DOVE AND THE BEE.

A Bee, whose business had led her to the brink of a purling stream, was snatched away by its circling eddy, and carried down its current. A Dove, pitying her distressed situation, cropped a twig from a tree, and dropt it before her in the water, by means of which the Bee saved herself, and got ashore. Not long after, a Fowler having a design upon the Dove, espied her sitting on a tree, and keeping out of her sight, was waiting the opportunity of shooting her. This the Bee perceiving, stung him on the ear, which made him give so sudden a start, that the Dove instantly took the alarm, and flew away.

APPLICATION.

WE ought ever with a ready zeal to extend our arm

2 x 2

to relieve a sinking friend from distress and danger, or endeavour to forewarn him against the wicked plots of his enemies. The benevolent man, from the most disinterested motives, will always be disposed to do good offices to all, and the grateful man will never forget to return them in kind, if it be possible; and there is not one good man in the world who may not on some occasion stand in need of the help of another. But gratitude is not very common among mankind. It is a heavenly spark, from which many virtues spring; and the source of pleasures which never enter the breast of the vile ingrate. The favours and kindnesses bestowed upon the grateful man, he cannot forget; those which are conferred upon the ungrateful, are lost: he concludes he would not have had them, if he had not deserved them.

THE SERPENT AND THE MAN.

A Child was playing in a meadow, and by chance trod upon a Serpent. The Serpent, in the fury of his passion, turned up and bit the Child with his venomous teeth, so that he died immediately. The Father of the Child, inspired with grief and revenge, took a weapon, and pursuing the Serpent, before he could get into his hole, struck at him and lopped off a piece of his tail. The next day, hoping by stratagem to finish his revenge, he brought to the Serpent's hole honey, and meal, and salt, and desired him to come forth, protesting that he only sought a reconciliation on both sides; but the Serpent answered him with a hiss to this purpose: In vain you attempt a reconciliation; for as long as the memory of the dead Child and the mangled tail subsists, it will be impossible for you and I to have any charity for each other.

APPLICATION.

WHEN persons have carried their differences to an
extreme length, it is in vain for them to think of re-
newing a cordial friendship; for in the heat of their
quarrel, many injuries must have been reciprocally
offered and received, which must tear asunder the
strongest bands of amity. The fury of their dissen-
tions may indeed subside, yet neither party can forgive
the wrongs which neither can forget. The consciousness of having provoked the resentment of another,
will dwell so continually upon the mind of the aggress-
or, that he cannot rest till he has finished his work,
and put it as much as possible out of his enemy's power
to make any return upon him; and the old proverb
will be verified which says, " The man who has injured you, will never forgive you." Morality bids us
forgive our enemies, and the voice of reason confirms
the same; but neither reason nor morality bids us enter into a friendship with, or repose a confidence in,
those who have injured us, and of whom we have a
bad opinion. We may resolve not to return ill-usage;
but ought never to put ourselves into the power of an
enemy.

THE HORSE AND THE OVER-LOADED ASS.

A clownish stupid Fellow, in travelling to market with his goods, loaded his Horse very lightly, and put a heavy burden upon his Ass, and was trudging along the road with them on foot. They had not travelled half-way to their journey's end, when the Ass felt greatly overpowered with the weight he carried, and begged the Horse would be so good as to assist him by taking a part of it upon his back, and lighten the grievous burden, assuring him that through weakness he was quite exhausted, and was ready to faint. No! said the Horse, keep your burden to yourself, it does not concern me. Upon hearing this cruel reply, the poor Ass dropped down, and soon expired. The Master then ungirded the pack-saddle, and awkwardly tried several ways to relieve his Ass, but all to no purpose; it was too late. When he perceived how matters stood, he took the whole burden and laid it upon the Horse, together with the skin of the dead Ass, and when he felt tired with walking, he also mounted himself. The Horse is said to have often muttered as he went along, Well, this is my proper punishment, for refusing to help my fellow-servant in the depth of his distress.

APPLICATION.

HE who has no compassion in his breast, is unworthy the title of a man; and the heart that feels no anguish at the misfortunes of others, nor a desire to relieve those who groan under a load of sorrow, is destitute of the very grounds and principles of virtue. The eye that has no tear for the griefs of a friend, is also blind to its own interest; for the burden of human affairs must be borne by some or other of us, and the duty, as well as the common necessity of helping one another, ought not to be shuffled off by the unworthy expression of " it is none of my business :" for the business of society is more or less the business of every man who lives in it; and he who permits his weak brother, for want of timely assistance, to sink under a greater weight than he is able to sustain, deserves to be punished for his cruelty, by being obliged to bear the whole of his own distressing burdens himself. The Fable also hints at the miseries which poor dumb useful animals undergo, from the injudicious management or cruel treatment of those under whose government they have the misfortune to fall. These kind of " hogs in armour" ought to be taught by their own sufferings, the benevolent text, that " A merciful man will be merciful to his beast."

THE HUSBANDMAN AND THE STORK.

A Husbandman having placed nets in his fields to catch the Rooks and the Geese, which came to feed upon the new-sown corn, found among his prisoners a single Stork, who happened to be in their company. The Stork pleaded hard for his life, and among other arguments, alleged that he was neither Goose nor Crow, but a poor harmless Stork, whose attachment to mankind, and his services to them in picking up noxious creatures, as well as fulfilling his duties to his aged parents, he trusted, were well known. All this may be true, says the Husbandman, for what I know; but as I have taken you in company with thieves, and in the same crime, you must also share the same fate with them.

2 Y

APPLICATION.

WHEN we become so abandoned to stupidity and a disregard of our reputation, as to keep bad company, however little we may be criminal in reality, we must expect the same censure and punishment as is due to the most notorious of our companions. The world will always form an idea of the character of every man from his associates: nor is this rule founded on wrong principles; for, generally speaking, those who are constant companions, are either drawn together by a similitude of manners and principles, or form such a similitude by daily commerce and conversation. If, therefore, we are tender of our reputation, we should be particularly delicate in the choice of our company, since some portion of their fame or infamy must unavoidably be reflected upon us. It is not enough to be virtuous ourselves, but we must be cautious not to associate with those who are devoted to vice: for, though we cannot confer any degree of our own credit upon them, we may suffer much discredit, and incur much danger, from mixing with such bad companions.

THE TRAVELLERS AND THE BEAR.

Two Men being to travel through a forest together, mutually engaged to stand by each other in any danger they might encounter on the way. They had not gone far, before a Bear rushed towards them out of a thicket; upon which, one of them, being a light nimble fellow, got up the branches of a tree, and kept out of sight. The other falling flat upon his face, and holding his breath, lay still, while the Bear came up and smelled at him, but not discovering any marks of life, he walked quietly away again to the place of his retreat, without doing the Man the least harm. When all was over, the Spark who had climbed the tree, came down to his Companion, and asked him, what the Bear said to him? for, says he, I took notice that he clapt his mouth very close to your ear.

Why, said the other, he advised me, for the future
never to place any confidence in such a faithless pol-
troon as you.

THERE is nothing in this world that can lighten
our burdens, in passing through it, or contribute more
to our happiness, than our knowing we have a true
friend, who will commiserate with and help us in our
misfortunes, and on whom we can rely in times of
difficulty and distress.   There are many, indeed, who,
with fair words, pretend to that character, and are
ever ready to offer their services when there is no occasion for their help.   But the real friend, like gold
from the furnace, shines forth in his true lustre, and
with heart and hand is ever ready to succour us, in
times of tribulation and peril.   It is on such only we
ought to place a confidence in any undertaking of importance; for the man who is wholly actuated by the
selfish unsocial principle of caring only for himself, is
not fit to be associated with others of a more generous
character; and he who will desert them in adversity
ought not to be made a partaker of the prosperity of
others.   It therefore behoves us diligently to examine
into the fidelity of those we have to deal with, before
we embark with them in any enterprise, in which our
lives and fortunes may be put to hazard by their breach
of faith.

THE FIGHTING COCKS.

AFTER a fierce battle between two Cocks for the sovereignty of the dunghill, one of them having beaten his antagonist, he that was vanquished slunk away and crept into a corner, where he for some time hid himself; but the conqueror flew up to a high place, and clapped his wings, crowing and proclaiming his victory. An Eagle, who was watching for his prey, saw him from afar off, and in the midst of his exultation darted down upon him, trussed him up, and bore him away. The vanquished Cock perceiving this, quitted the place of his retreat, and shaking his feathers and throwing off all remembrance of his late disgrace, returned to the dunghill, and gallanted the Hens, as if nothing had happened.

APPLICATION.

THIS Fable shews us the impropriety and inconvenience of running into extremes, and teaches us, that under all the various and sudden vicissitudes of human life, we ought to bear success with moderation, and misfortune with fortitude and equinamity; to repress immoderate exultation, and unmanly despair. Much of our happiness depends upon keeping an even balance in our words and actions, and in not suffering circumstances to mount us too high in time of prosperity, nor to sink us too low with the weight of adverse fortune. A wise man will not place too high a value on blessings which he knows to be no more than temporary; nor will he repine at evils, whose duration may perhaps be but short, and cannot be eternal. He will submit himself with humility and resignation to the decrees of providence, and the will of heaven. In prosperity, the fear of evil will check the insolence of triumph; and in adversity, the hope of good will sustain his spirit, and teach him to endure his misfortunes with constancy and fortitude.

THE WILD AND THE TAME GEESE.

A flock of Wild Geese and a parcel of Tame ones used often to feed together in a corn field. At last, the Owner of the corn, with his servants, coming up-on them of a sudden, surprised them in the very fact, and the Tame Geese being heavy, and fat full-bodied creatures, were most of them sufferers; but the wild ones being thin and light, easily flew away.

APPLICATION.

When the enemy comes to make a seizure, they are sure to suffer most whose circumstances are the richest and fattest. In any case of persecution, mo-ney hangs like a dead weight about a man; and we never feel gold so heavy as when we are endeavouring

to make off with it. Great wealth has many cares
annexed to it, with which the poor and needy are not
afflicted. A competency to supply the necessities of
nature, and the wants of old age, is indeed to be desired ; but we should rather endeavour to contract our
wants, than to multiply them, and not too eagerly
grasp at the augmentation of our possessions, which
will increase our cares by adding to our danger. Persons of small fortune have as much reason to be contented as the rich : their situation is full as happy, considered altogether, for if they are deprived of some of
the gratifications which the rich enjoy, they are also
exempted from many troubles and uneasinesses neces-
sarily cleaving to riches.

THE FROGS AND THE MICE.

THE Frogs and the Mice, who inhabited part of a most extensive fen, (of which there remained unoccupied sufficient room to hold many whole nations of both) could not agree with each other so as to live in peace : many bitter disputes arose between them about the right to particular pools, and their tuft-covered margins. At length, national jealousies and animosities arose to such a height, that each claimed the sovereignty of the whole fen, and the most rancorous war was waged between them, in order to settle, by force of arms, their respective pretensions. While their hostile armies were drawn up in battle array, on a plain of several square yards in extent, protected on both flanks and rear by dark pools and gloomy forests of sedges, reeds, and bulrushes, their two chieftains

2 z

advanced to meet each other, and to it they fell as
fierce as tigers. While these two combatants were thus
engaged, a Kite sailing in the air, beheld them from a
great distance, and darting down upon them, instantly
bore them off in his talons; while the field of battle
presented a delicious repast to some Ravens, who had
chanced to spy the movements of these hostile armies.

APPLICATION.

THE leading feature in the character of men, in all
ages of the world, has ever been self-interest; and
when this is not kept within due bounds, by a just sense
of morality and honour, their bad passions are let
loose, and money, power, or dominion, are the chief
objects they keep in view. When men thus depraved,
have long soared above restraint, and their numbers
and power become predominant in a nation, the ac-
cumulation of their wickedness hurries them blindly
on to break out into offensive wars with other nations,
on the most frivolous pretences, and rapine, plunder, and innumerable murders succeed, by which humanity is outraged, and the fair face of nature is
deluged with blood. " Peace is the natural happy
state of man, and war is his disgrace." The mighty
among the Frogs and Mice attend not to this: they
strut and exult for a time; but their pride, tyranny, and
injustice, will have an end: for opposed to these vices
are the attributes of Omnipotence, and they are eternal.
It often happens (as in the case of the combatants in
the Fable) that when national depravity has attained
its height, the Kites and Ravens of other regions are
invited forth, and made the instruments of a just
retribution.

THE FOWLER AND THE LARK.

A Fowler set his snares to catch birds in the open field. A Lark was caught; and finding herself entangled, could not forbear lamenting her hard fate. Ah! woe is me, says she, what crime have I committed that man should be plotting my destruction? I have not taken either his silver or gold, or any thing of value to him; and while other rapacious birds deal about destruction and go unpunished, I must die for only picking up a single grain of corn.

APPLICATION.

The irregular administration of justice in the world, is indeed a melancholy subject to think of. A poor fellow shall be hanged for stealing a sheep, perhaps to keep his family from starving; while one, who is already great and opulent, will not scruple to add to his overflowing wealth by the most bare-faced peculation upon the public, and yet shall escape punishment, and even censure, through powerful interest with those who ought to be his judges, but allow themselves to be swayed by the splendour of his connections, or corrupted by his money. When justice is intrusted in such hands, then shall we see the description given by one of our satirical poets, of a corrupt court of law, realized. He calls it a place,

Where little villains must submit to fate,
That great ones may enjoy the world in state.

However, let no one, who violates the law, rest his defence on this plea; for though crimes, committed by his superiors, ought not to escape with impunity, yet his own nevertheless deserve punishment. Hence we may also draw a hint, not unworthy of our attention, to endeavour to preserve our own integrity, unshaken in the midst of iniquity, and to shew ourselves unstained by the corruption even of the worst of times.

THE SHEPHERD TURNED MERCHANT.

A Shepherd was feeding his flock, on a very fine day, near the sea-side. The beauty of the weather, the smoothness of the water, and the ships with spreading sails floating along its surface, formed altogether so charming a scene, that he lost all relish for a pastoral life; and lured also by the prospect of gain, he determined to quit an employment, which he now despised as yielding neither honour nor profit. He quickly sold off his flocks, and commenced merchant adventurer; and ere long, he embarked with his whole property on the ocean. The ship had not long been at sea before a dreadful tempest arose, which wrecked her and all her cargo; but our merchant and the crew were fortunate enough to escape with their lives. The adventurer having thus lost his all, returned to his former farm, and was glad to hire himself to the man who had bought his stock, to attend the sheep which were once his own. One day, as he sat meditating upon the change that had happened, and viewing the sea calm and unruffled as before, Ah! says he, thou deceitful tempting element, experience has made me so wise, that if I should again acquire a property, I will never more trust it upon thy faithless bosom.

APPLICATION.

This Fable is intended to put men of fickle unsettled minds upon their guard against that propensity which often inclines them so strongly to shifting and changing, and leads them to imagine they would be happier in any profession than the one to which they have been brought up. By this disposition they are led away from an honest competency, to adventure their all upon untried schemes, in the hope of bettering their condition. But men of this wavering temper, who are comfortably settled in the world, would do well to reflect, before they change their situation, and rashly venture, perhaps, the acquisitions of their whole life, on projects, the failure of which may subject them to great calamities, which will be the more intolerable to bear, as they will not have adverse fortune to blame, but merely their own folly. Of this truth, experience will convince them when it is too late.

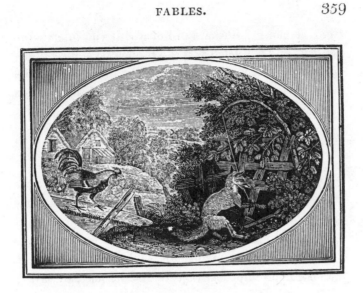

THE COCK AND THE FOX.

A Fox, in one of his early visits to the farm-yard, happened to be caught in a springe, which had been set for that very purpose; and while he was struggling to escape, he was observed by the Cock, who, with his Hens, was feeding near the place. The Cock, dreading so dangerous a foe, approached him with the utmost caution. Reynard no sooner cast his eye upon him, than with all the smooth and designing artifice imaginable, thus addressed him. My dear friend, says he, you see what an unfortunate accident has befallen me here, and all upon your account, for not having heard you crow for a long time past, I was resolved on my way homeward to pay you a friendly visit; I therefore beg you will bring me something to cut this tormenting wire, or at least be so good as to conceal my misfortune till I have knawed it asunder. Yes, said the

Cock, I can guess what kind of a visit you intended to pay me, and will fetch you the proper assistance immediately. He then hastened and told the Farmer, who instantly went to the place, and knocked the Fox on the head.

APPLICATION.

WHEN the innocent fall into misfortune, it is the part of a generous and brave spirit to contribute as far as possible to their relief; and there is no quality of mind more amiable than that of tenderly feeling for the distressed: but we ought not to let our compassion flow out upon improper objects, lest we may, by saving a villain, be doing an act of injustice to the community. When wicked men are entrapped in their own pernicious schemes, and laid hold of by the arm of justice, it is a misplaced lenity to endeavour to screen or protect them from it, as by letting them loose to continue their depredations, we become the advocates for their crimes, and in some degree partakers in their enormities.

THE YOUNG MAN AND HIS CAT.

A certain Young Man used to play with a beautiful Cat, of which he grew so fond, that at last he fell in love with it to such a degree, that he could rest neither night nor day for the excess of his passion. In this condition he prayed to Venus, the goddess of beauty, to pity and relieve his pain. The good-natured goddess was propitious, and heard his prayers; and the Cat, which he held in his arms, was instantly transformed into a beautiful Young Woman. The Youth was transported with joy, and married her that very day. At night, while they were in bed, the bride unfortunately heard a mouse behind the hangings, and sprang from the arms of her lover to pursue it: the Youth was ashamed, and Venus offended, to see her sacred rites thus profaned by such unbecoming behaviour; and perceiving that her new convert, though a woman

3 A

in outward appearance, was a Cat in her heart, she caused her to return to her old form again, that her manners and person might be suitable to each other.

This Fable, however extravagant and unnatural in its composition, is intended to depicture and check the blind instinctive ardour of the passion of love, the transports of which cover all imperfections, so that its devotees consider neither quality nor merit. It is like an idol of our own creating, which we fashion into whatever figure or shape we please, and then run mad for it. The Fable also shews that

" No charm can raise from dirt a grov'ling mind ;"

And that people of a low turn of spirit and mean education, cannot change their principles by changing their situation : for in the midst of splendour and magnificence, they still retain the same narrow sentiments, and seldom fail to betray, by some dirty action, their original baseness, which no embroidery can conceal ; and though fortune has been pleased to lift them out of the mire, we still see the silly awkward blockheads displaying their lack of mind and education through all their ensigns of dignity. If any thing more need be added, it can only be with a view of more plainly putting inexperienced youth on their guard against making inconsiderate connections, lest they take a Cat into their bosom, instead of an amiable consort and companion for life.

THE FOWLER AND THE PARTRIDGE.

A Fowler having taken a Partridge in his nets, the bird begged hard for a reprieve, and promised the man, if he would let him go, to decoy the other Partridges into his snares. No, replies the Fowler, if I had before been undetermined what to do with you, now you have condemned yourself by your own words: for he who is such a scoundrel as to offer to betray his friends, to save himself, deserves if possible worse than death.

APPLICATION.

To betray our friends is one of the blackest of crimes; and however much traitors may suppose they recommend themselves by their successful acts of treachery, they will find that those who employ them as useful instruments in any dirty business of faction or party, are shocked at the baseness of their minds; and however convenient it may be to " like the treason, the traitor will be despised." History furnishes us with many instances of kings and great men who have punished the actors of treachery with death, though the part they acted had been so conducive to their interests as to give them a victory, or perhaps the quiet possession of a throne: nor can princes pursue a more just maxim than this, for a traitor is a villain, and sticks at nothing to promote his own selfish ends. He that will betray one master for a bribe, will betray another on the same account. It is therefore impolitic in any state to suffer such wretches to live under its protection. Since then this maxim is so good, and likely at all times to be acted upon, what stupid rogues must they be who undertake such precarious dirty work !

THE BLIND MAN AND THE LAME.

A blind Man and a lame Man happening to come at the same time to a piece of very bad road, the former begged of the latter that he would be so kind as to guide him through the difficulty. How can I do that, said the lame Man, since I am scarcely able to drag myself along? But as you appear to be very strong, if you will carry me, we will seek our fortunes together. It will then be my interest to warn you against any thing that may obstruct your way; your feet shall be my feet, and my eyes your's. With all my heart, replied the blind Man; let us mutually serve each other. So, taking his lame companion on his back, they by means of this union travelled on with safety and pleasure.

APPLICATION.

THERE is no such thing as absolute independence, in a state of society, and the defects and weaknesses of individuals form the cement by which it is bound together. All men have their imperfections and wants, and must help each other as a matter of expediency as well as virtue; for Providence has so ordered things in this life, that like the blind man and the lame in the Fable, we may be serviceable to each other in almost every instance. What one man wants another supplies. Without these failings there would be neither friendship nor company; so that it is our interest to be both charitable and sociable, when our very wants and necessities are converted by Providence into blessings. The whole race of mankind ought indeed to be but so many members of the same body; and in contributing to the ease and convenience of each other, we are not only serviceable to the whole, but kind to ourselves.

THE LION, THE WOLF, AND THE DOG.

A Lion having seized upon a Doe, while he was standing over his prize, a Wolf stepped up to him, and impudently claimed to go halves. No! said the Lion, you are too apt to take what is not your due. I therefore shall never have any thing to do with you, and I peremptorily insist on your immediate departure out of my sight. A poor honest Dog, who happened to be passing, and heard what was going on, modestly withdrew, intending to go about another way. Upon which the Lion kindly invited him to come forward and partake with him of the feast, to which his modesty had given him so good a title.

APPLICATION.

THERE is something in modesty which ought ever

strongly to prepossess us in favour of those persons in whose nature it is interwoven; and men of discerning and generous minds have a pleasure in discovering it, and in bringing into notice the worthy man, who is diffident of his merit, and cannot prevail upon himself to challenge the praise or tribute he deserves. It is, however, to be lamented, that such patrons are not very numerous, and that the assuming arrogance and teasing importunities of the greedy forward man should so commonly succeed in attaining his ends, while modesty in silence starves unnoticed, and is for ever poor. Were men in exalted stations of life to pay more attention to the importance of this, and endeavour to discover modest worth, to draw merit from the shade, and virtue from obscurity, and distribute their patronage and their favours to such only, their own affairs, as well as those of the public, would be better managed, and the difference between the conduct of upstart pride and sensible plain honesty would soon shew itself in its true unvarnished colours.

THE ASS EATING THISTLES.

An Ass was loaded with provisions of several sorts, which he was carrying home for a grand entertainment. By the way, he met with a fine large Thistle, and being very hungry, immediately eat it up, which, while he was doing, he entered into this reflection: How many greedy epicures would think themselves happy amidst such a variety of delicate viands as I now carry! But to me, this bitter prickly Thistle is more savory and relishing than the most exquisite and sumptuous banquet.

APPLICATION.

Temperance and exercise may be regarded as the constituents of natural luxury. It is not in the power

of the whole art of cookery, to give such an exquisite
relish and seasoning to a dish, as these two will confer
on the plainest fare. Indolent epicures have no true
taste: they subsist entirely by whets and provocatives
of appetite; but he whose stomach is braced and
strengthened by exercise, has a whet within himself,
which adds a poignancy to every morsel that he eats.
Providence seems to have carved out its blessings with
an equal hand, and what it has denied to the poor in
one way, it has amply supplied them with in another:
if it have withheld riches, it has given them a greater
store of health; and if it have refused them the means
of luxury, it has at least formed them with the capacity of living as happily without it. And it may further be observed, that if we except hereditary diseases,
almost every other ailment may be laid to the account
of indolence, intemperance, or anxiety of mind.

THE DOG AND THE CAT.

NEVER were two creatures happier together than a Dog and a Cat, reared in the same house from the time of their birth. They were so kind, so gamesome, and diverting, that it was half the entertainment of the family to see the gambols and love tricks that passed between them. Still it was observed, that at meal-times, when scraps fell from the table, or a tit-bit was thrown to them, they would be snarling and spitting at one another like the bitterest foes.

APPLICATION.

THIS Fable is too true a picture of the practices and friendships of the world. We first enter into agreeable conversations, contract likings, and form

close intimacies and connections, which one would
think nothing could ever break up ; but clashing interests at length come in the way, and dissolve the
charm.   An unreasonable desire to engross more than
we can enjoy, is the bone of contention, which in
greater or less degrees sets mankind together by the
ears.   A jealous thought, a mistaken word or look,
is then sufficient to cancel all former bonds: the league
is broken, and the farce concludes like the Dog and
the Cat in the Fable, with biting and scratching out
one another's eyes.   The same kind of over-grasp-
ing selfishness which operates so powerfully upon and
blinds individuals, may with equal truth be charged
against all public associations or societies of men, from
the greatest to the least, when they are under the influence of that mistaken patriotism, which, instead of
applying its powers to the improvement of what they
already possess, seeks aggrandizement by engrossing
the colonies or privileges of their less powerful neighbours.

THE TRUMPETER TAKEN PRISONER.

A Trumpeter, being taken prisoner in battle, begged hard for quarter, declaring his innocence, and protesting, that he neither had killed nor could kill any man, bearing no arms but his trumpet, which he was obliged to sound at the word of command. For that reason, replied his enemies, we are determined not to spare you; for though you yourself never fight, yet, with that wicked instrument of yours, you blow up animosity among other people, and so become the cause of much bloodshed.

APPLICATION.

THE fomenter of mischief is at least as culpable as he who puts it in execution. A man may be guilty of murder, who never has handled a sword or pulled a trigger, or lifted up his arm with any mischievous weapon. There is a little incendiary called the tongue, which is more venomous than a poisoned arrow, and more killing than a two-edged sword. The moral of the Fable therefore is this, that if in any civil insurrection, the persons taken in arms against the government deserve to die, much more do they whose devilish tongues or pens gave birth to the sedition, and excited the tumult. The Fable is also equally applicable to those evil counsellors, who excite corrupt or wicked governments to sap and undermine, and then to overturn the just laws and liberties of a whole people; or involve them in cruel offensive wars, in which they cause thousands upon thousands of swords to be drawn, and whole armies of men to be cut in pieces, while they themselves coolly sit out of danger, and calculate the gains they derive from the wide-spreading desolation. War is the most horrid custom that ever resulted from human wickedness, and is caused only by the ignorance of the people, or the wickedness of governments.

THE BOYS AND THE FROGS.

A company of idle Boys used to assemble on the margin of a lake, inhabited by a great number of Frogs, and divert themselves by throwing vollies of stones into the water, to the great annoyance and danger of the poor terrified Frogs, who were thus pelted to death as soon as any of them put up their heads. At length, one of the boldest of the Frogs ventured, in behalf of the whole community, to croak out their complaints. Ah, my Boys, said he, why will you learn so soon the cruel practices of your race? Consider, I beseech you, that though this may be sport to you, it is death to us !

APPLICATION.

THIS Fable shews the propensity of unguided youth to do evil, and points out the need of inculcating be-

nignity of conduct upon their minds, and giving them
a direction towards a manly and generous humanity,
which in manhood will shew itself in actions and ha-
bits that cannot fail to do honour to themselves, and
qualify them for any office in the service of their country.   The contrary of all this will be found to predo-
minate in society, when youth are suffered to go on
with impunity, in indulging their wicked inclinations
for cruelty, by which their minds are hardened and
debased.   This hard-heartedness in boys will grow into brutality and tyranny in man; and that cruelty
which was at first inflicted upon poor dumb animals,
will soon shew itself upon their fellows.   The great
man of this cast will tyrannize over those below him :
these again will shew the same hateful disposition to
their dependants, and so downwards to the lowest,
who, guided only by ignorance, will give vent to their
natural baseness, by goading and distressing the poor
animals which are wretchedly toiling in their service.

FINIS.

NEWCASTLE : PRINTED BY EDWARD WALKER.